PRAISE FOR
SEVEN FIGURE FIRM

"For any advisor who is looking to build a true business—as opposed to managing a basic practice—Erin Botsford's book is a must-read. Erin is one of the wealth management industry's best examples of how an advisor with a CEO state of mind can ignite structured, strategic, and sustainable growth. Her latest book should be on the desk of any advisor who is looking for a plan and a process that can propel their firm to the next level."

—Mark Bruno, Managing Director, Emigrant Partners

"It's not often that you find a successful person willing to reveal the secret sauce of their success. But that is what Erin Botsford has done in her latest book *Seven Figure Firm: How to Build a Financial Services Business that Grows Itself*. Often financial advisers struggle to transform their successful practice into a self-sustaining business. Ms. Botsford explains how she did it and offers practical guidelines of how to replicate her success, right down to the details of where to seat clients in an initial meeting and why it is important to keep track of their coffee, tea, or Coke preference. In an era of robo-advisors, building a brand to differentiate your services is key and establishing systems to provide a consistently superior client experience is the equivalent of building the golden arches of a successful financial services firm."

—Mary Beth Franklin, CFP, Contributing Editor, *Investment News*

"Erin Botsford has never accepted the concept of a glass ceiling and as a result, she turned a business plan into a financial planning practice that grew to become one of the most successful financial planning businesses in the country. It's powerful reading. Erin's ability to convert a practice into a business, one that thrives without her micromanaging, is a skill to be emulated by others."

—Joby Gruber, CEO, Beacon Global Advisors

"Advisor practices hit the 'ceiling of complexity' at around the $200,000 revenue level, with most never breaking through or discovering the highly prized code of a seven-figure firm. Erin Botsford, CFP industry rock star and *Barron's* Top 100 Independent Advisor, opens up about what really works to break through that ceiling of complexity, sustain an ideal life, and practice with a seven-figure firm."

—SteVan H. Gates, CRPC®, Private Wealth Advisor, Allegis Wealth Management

"I seldom enjoy these types of books, but this was a great read! Erin is the Queen of Implementation. She has not only created the systems and processes to ensure success, but she's actually applied them in her own practice with outstanding results."

—Jeffrey A. Concepcion, ChFC, President & CEO, Stratos Wealth Partners, Ltd.

"I have had the privilege of consulting with hundreds of advisors, including Erin Botsford, regarding practice management strategies throughout my seventeen-year career in the financial services industry. Erin has created a formula and road map to drive a practice to new levels of productivity and revenue. Her journey, as stated in her book, has been both compelling and inspiring, one that advisors both new to the business and with years of experience must read. They say, 'Experience is the best teacher,' and Erin's new book delivers."

—Peter M. Jawidzik, VP, Business Solutions, LPL Financial

"Erin Botsford has learned and done what it takes to create a dream life as a financial advisor. What an advantage to those aspiring to the same to have access to the wealth of wisdom, encouragement, and sage, actionable advice on all aspects of creating an extraordinary practice that she shares in this book."

—Dan Sullivan, Founder, The Strategic Coach, Inc.

"In my two decades in the financial service industry, I've met none better than Erin Botsford. If you are a wholesaler, buy this book for your financial advisors! It's a treasure chest of information."

—Nathan Medin, Senior Partner, Universal Financial Consultants

"At a time when the financial advisory profession is experiencing a dearth of talent, Erin Botsford shares her personal story describing how she turned headwinds into tailwinds to create a business that has been personally fulfilling, financially rewarding, and impactful on the clients and employees with whom she's worked. This book is an insightful read for anyone considering the business of providing financial advice as a career and is an especially inspiring tale for women considering this profession. Erin is an example of how to conquer the unconscious bias of others and one's own fear of failure. Erin not only touches on the emotion of building a business, but on the practical aspects of executing a plan that takes emotion out of the equation. *Seven Figure Firm* is a worthy read for financial professionals seeking ideas and examples of how to transform from a managing business to running a true business enterprise."

—Mark Tibergien, Retired CEO,
Pershing Advisor Solutions, a BNY Mellon company

"The best in the business are coachable, curious, and committed to building legacy businesses built for generations of clients and team members. Having coached Erin and her team, their focus on a lifetime of learning, changing, improving, and sharing with others is intentional. Their business is certainly one every advisor can learn from."

—Ray Sclafani, CEO, ClientWise®

"If you are looking for the how and not just the why of building a successful practice, this is the book for you. Erin focuses on teaching you her process, and the results will follow. We know how much Erin cares about people and how committed she is to doing meaningful work. The *Seven Figure Firm* approach is clear evidence that Erin's principles drive superior performance."

—Roseann (Ro) Morrison & Chris Dungworth,
Managing Partners, Ro Morrison & Associates

$even
FIGURE
FIRM

SECOND EDITION

$even FIGURE FIRM

How *to* Build *a*
Financial Services Business
that Grows Itself

Second Edition

ERIN BOTSFORD

RIVER GROVE
BOOKS

Published by River Grove Books

Austin, TX
www.rivergrovebooks.com

Distributed by River Grove Books

Design and composition by Greenleaf Book Group
Cover design by Greenleaf Book Group
Cover image©iStockphoto.com/Varijanta;
NUMAX3D, 2016. Used under license from Shutterstock.com

Publisher's Cataloging-in-Publication data is available.

Paperback ISBN: 978-1-63299-836-1

Hardcover ISBN: 978-1-63299-837-8

eBook ISBN: 978-1-63299-838-5

Second Edition

This book is dedicated to Kevin William Botsford, a true American patriot, a loving husband, a dedicated father, and my one and only child. To say I am proud of the man he has become would be an understatement. The most meaningful moments of my life have been those spent nurturing his character and, more importantly, his soul.

CONTENTS

FOREWORD

Henry David Thoreau famously said, "Go confidently in the direction of your dreams. Live the life you've imagined." Erin Botsford has figured out a strategy to do just that for herself, her family, friends, clients, and even orphans in Africa.

She didn't have a guidebook. She has done it on her own by trial and error with dogged determination, hard work, ingenuity, enthusiasm, and empathy.

The wonderful thing about Erin is she is sharing her approach with the rest of us, so anyone running a business (and let's face it, we are all running a business called "ourselves") can live the life they've imagined too.

I met Erin several years ago when I interviewed her on *Consuelo Mack WealthTrack*, my national weekly investment program on public television. She had come highly recommended by a close friend and fellow journalist, Mary Beth Franklin, who was personally and professionally impressed by Erin's trademarked investment philosophy "Lifestyle Driven Investing™." Her philosophy has since caught on industrywide because it makes so much sense.

Erin had been named to the *Barron's* Top 100 Independent Financial Advisors list, as well as its Top 100 Women Financial

Advisors. She had also just come out with her first book: *The Big Retirement Risk: Running Out of Money Before You Run Out of Time*, which made the best-seller list.

I read the book and researched Erin, and I came away very impressed by both. We invited her to appear as a guest on *WealthTrack*, the first of what would and will be many appearances.

I have always been fascinated by the stories of very successful people. What motivates them, what did it take to get there, and what could I learn from them to apply in my own life? *Seven Figure Firm* is an amazing story about a woman who has created an extraordinary life for herself and others, that now extends to hands-on global philanthropy. It is a page-turner that I didn't want to put down. I read it pretty much in a single day.

As a pre-teen, Erin's family lost everything when her father died suddenly, leaving them without savings or insurance. The family suffered another blow when, through no fault of her own, Erin was involved in a fatal car accident with a motorcyclist at the age of sixteen. Both experiences taught her a searing lesson: Without money you have few, if any, choices. At an early age, she resolved never to be without money again and to learn everything she could about finance and investing. She has done that and so much more.

In *Seven Figure Firm*, Erin tells her remarkable story about achieving financial security for herself and her family while building a thriving business that she has intentionally designed to run without her. This strategy enables her to devote more time to spreading the word about Lifestyle Driven Investing™, visiting with her grandchildren, and focusing on her philanthropic work.

Erin helps with causes from serving returning military veterans to providing water wells, orphan homes, and other humanitarian aid to women and children in Africa.

Although this book was written for financial advisors, it has been an eye-opener for me. It provides excellent advice for other entrepreneurs who want their businesses to grow and last. Erin is making a huge difference in many lives. *Seven Figure Firm* can help you do the same and live the life you've imagined.

Consuelo Mack

Anchor and Executive Producer

Consuelo Mack WealthTrack

January 2024

ACKNOWLEDGMENTS

I would like to thank my husband, Bob Botsford, who has stood by me in all my business endeavors and wild adventures. His steadfast and unwavering belief in me has been the rock upon which I built both my businesses and my life. Not only did he have a successful career as an airline pilot, but he has also been the CFO for both my financial services company and our advisor training company. Bob has been an integral part of everything in my life.

I would like to thank my former business partner, Kay Lynn Mayhue, who was integral to the success of our financial services firm. I still remember the day many years ago when I came home all fired up from a very inspiring day with a successful advisor and announced I was going to go build a large financial planning firm. I told Kay Lynn I needed her to run the business while I went out and brought in new clients and sold the philosophy of our firm. I asked if she would be willing to do that; quite to my surprise, she said, "Yes," and she did so in a consistently excellent way. I could have never predicted that our efforts would result in such amazing success. To her credit, she kept the wheels from coming off more times than I would care to admit! When you move as fast as we did over the years, you better have someone like Kay Lynn by your side with a wrench in her hand!

Much gratitude is also owed to my former team at Botsford Financial Group, who believed in me and helped me create a very successful firm. Their collective efforts allowed us to build a business that ran like a well-oiled machine and did so without my day-to-day involvement. Their unwavering loyalty gave me the peace of mind to explore new business ideas, create my training program—the Elite Advisor Success System™—and pursue my charitable endeavors.

To Mike Sbonik, Blake Hammerton, and Jamison Hammerton, who took my vision for creating an advisor training program and brought it to life. Their complementary talents and unwavering dedication have allowed many to benefit from what we collectively built.

I thank God for giving me an amazing family. My son, Kevin, has been a constant source of inspiration to me. His love for our country found him in the heat of battle on more than two hundred combat missions in the US Air Force. Never once complaining, he spent many holidays on the battlefield while the rest of us enjoyed our turkeys and Christmas trees. His wife, Kristin, brilliant in her own right, held down the fort and made the sacrifices asked of a military spouse. Not only is she a praying wife, but she is also a great mom to my grandsons, Cooper, Carson, and Christian. No words can describe my love for these three boys, who thrill me with their very being. I pray they grow to be men of God, following in the footsteps of a great legacy of Godly men.

Let me also acknowledge my extended family of McGowans

and Botsfords. Your unwavering love and support, often from afar, has been a source of constant encouragement. I am also grateful to my friends who have stood by me through thick and thin and, at times, told me the truth. You have helped me keep balance in my life. Thank you for being my social directors, the source of much laughter, and more importantly, my prayer warriors.

Much gratitude, as well, to Dan Sullivan and Babs Smith, creators and founders of The Strategic Coach Program, who played instrumental roles in my business success. My all-time favorite saying from Dan is, "Always keep your future bigger than your past."

I have attempted to live my life true to that motto.

I would be remiss if I didn't also mention Hal Burleson, my first mentor and a good friend. He did so much to help me succeed in my earliest years in the business. I will never forget the way Hal would stop and put his pencil down whenever I had a question for him. His generosity of spirit and his abundance mentality are forever embedded in my soul.

Although this book is designed and dedicated for financial advisors, I am forever grateful to the clients of Botsford Financial who took a chance on me, even when I was a young female in the South. The hardest decision in the world is trusting someone else with your health or your money. I am honored that so many chose to trust me with their finances, their future, and their legacy. It was an honor to serve each and every one of them. It is especially rewarding to know they are still being served by my former firm.

And finally, to the financial advisors who took a leap of faith and enrolled in my Elite Advisor Success System™ because they decided they too wanted to build the businesses of their dreams.

As I tell them every day, their success is the oxygen that feeds my soul. It has been such an honor to train and mentor so many fine, dedicated advisors.

INTRODUCTION
Succeed—ME?

I am probably the least likely person ever to have succeeded in the financial services business.

And yet I did. Beyond my *wildest* dreams.

I still recall that July day many years ago when I sat down to meet with my new boss. He was the one who hired me for my first job as a stockbroker. I had just spent three weeks training in the home office, and now I was back in his office, ready to discuss the business plan that would launch me into my new career. I had worked so hard to get the business plan just right and was excited to share it with him.

My boss sat back quietly and listened to my presentation.

When I was done, he said, "Honey, I have to give you a lot of credit. You have come up with an incredible business plan, probably better than most I have seen (truth be told, it was the only business plan he'd ever seen). But I have to tell you up front—this is never going to work. You're a sure recipe for disaster."

I was almost too stunned to speak. I managed to compose myself enough to ask him why he assumed I would fail.

"Because you are young, you are a female, and this is the South. It's never going to work," he said.

He wasn't trying to be mean. After all, he had hired me and was willing to give me a shot. It's just that he couldn't help thinking like the male chauvinist he was. He was very much a product of his day.

Granted, my boss was right about a few things. I was young. I was female. I was in the South.

I had a few other strikes against me too.

I had no connections. My husband was in the US Air Force—he was an F-15 fighter pilot—and because of the requirements of his training, we had moved seventeen times in the first fourteen years we were married. We had recently moved back to the United States, and I knew very few people in my community.

I didn't come from money. My dad died when I was eleven, leaving my family destitute.

I was also a mom. My son was only five years old when I started, and he needed looking after when the school day was done.

But that man wasn't right about me.

I told myself that failure wasn't an option.

There was NO way I was going to fail. That man's words fueled a fire inside my belly.

. . .

Instead, I became the founder and CEO of Botsford Financial Group, a boutique planning firm with offices in Dallas, Texas, and Atlanta, Georgia. I became a *Barron's* Top 100 Independent

Advisor[1] and a *Barron's* Top 100 Women's Financial Advisor. I became known for a trademarked investment philosophy called Lifestyle Driven Investing™. I am invited to give keynote addresses across the country. And I am sought after for my ability to teach, train, and motivate advisors.

In fact, when I was asked to train the twenty-five top producers of a major broker/dealer, their average production was up over more than twenty-five percent the following year. In addition, through our Elite Advisor Success System™, the average advisor who goes through this program has been up an average of forty-four percent in their first year!

I am convinced if someone like me can create this level of success in the financial services industry, then so can you.

But it takes more than drive. And that is why I wrote this book. I want to share the tools, systems, strategies, and mindset I used to propel my business to the top.

Consider this: If you had chosen to become a doctor, lawyer, or CPA, instead of a financial advisor, you would have a clear, defined pathway to professional success. Generally speaking, the people who are drawn to such careers tend to be comfortable fitting into formalized, hierarchical structures. Hence, their willingness to complete the additional years of post-secondary education. These are people who tend to be comfortable following the prescribed paths that lead an associate to partner and a partner to senior

---

1.   *Barron's* ranking of the top 100 financial advisors is based on assets under management, revenue generated for the advisors' firms, and the quality of advisors' practices.

partner. Not so for most financial advisors. The barriers to entry are relatively few for financial advisors.

Our profession attracts "rugged individualists" with an entrepreneurial nature. Because of our entrepreneurial nature, we tend to be less accepting of structured paths to success. We seem almost fated to reinvent the wheel as we figure out how to achieve career success on our own.

Not so long ago, you could enter the business through just two gates. You could enter through the insurance industry gate or become a stockbroker through the wire house portal. (I entered through the stock-brokerage portal.) After entering through one of these gates, you were given two types of training: sales training and product knowledge training. Once you left the home office and passed all your exams, you were left to sink or swim based on your own ingenuity and internal fortitude.

Now there are more points of entry. Today, for instance, more and more universities are turning out graduates in the field of financial planning. These graduates seem to be a new breed of financial advisors. They want to move into structures that are akin to those in the big accounting firms, where there are job descriptions, training programs, and pathways to partnership. However, the reality is that they will go to work for "rugged individualists" who expect their new employee to be totally comfortable with on-the-job training. In some cases, they are expected to learn by osmosis. I can relate. I had to learn much of what I know today the hard way—by trial and error and sheer determination.

Certainly, that's a tough road.

Fortunately, there's an easier, surer route to success. Learn from someone who has been in your shoes and has figured out what works and what doesn't. I have to assume if you're reading this book, you want to achieve an even higher level of success and you're ready and willing to learn.

With that in mind, let me begin by sharing three essential pieces of advice. First, realize that prospecting is forever. *You can never stop prospecting.* I wish I had known that from the beginning. For some reason, I had it in my head that all I had to do was prospect for seven years and new clients would magically find their way to my doorstep from that point forward. I didn't realize my entire career would be dominated by business development activities. I think I would have been okay with that realization; I just didn't know it early on in my career.

Second, *learn to think like a business owner instead of a product salesperson.* I wish someone had made that clear at the start as well. Yes, I had heard vague talk about "building my own business," but it didn't occur to me that a business was an entity that should be able to run on its own, without the day-to-day involvement of its owner. I learned later that if the business relied upon me, it really wasn't a business. Rather, I had just bought myself a job.

When you break it down, there are essentially five keys to success in this business—(1) Having a Mindset of Achievement, (2) Being Able to Identify and Close Your Ideal Client, (3) Prospecting and Marketing for Your Ideal Client, (4) Leveraging Your Time, and (5) Creating Systems and Processes to Run Your Business. I'll talk about each of these keys at length in the chapters that follow. I'll explain how to use each key to organize your own financial services business. I'll also discuss the personal discipline it takes to harness all five of the above keys. Finally, we'll talk about planning your exit, because the key to a successful sale or exit needs to be planned long before you ever pull the trigger.

There is no doubt in my mind that if you use even a few of my tips to organize your business, then you, too, can succeed beyond your wildest dreams. As I said before, if someone like me can do it, then so can you!

CHAPTER 1

FROM BROKE TO
BARRON'S TOP 100

E very time I am asked to give an industry speech, I always
make a point of telling my personal story as well as my
business story. Why? Because I am quite aware that everyone in
the audience is sizing me up. They want to know what advantages
I had that allowed me to become so successful. After all, I'm the
one at the podium. It's just human nature to wonder what "edge"
I had and what connections were available to me.

What I have learned over the years is that if I don't tell the audience my story, some audience members will make one up about
me and it's usually nowhere near the truth.

MY PERSONAL STORY

What gave me the inner conviction as a young stockbroker to
know I could succeed—even when the man who hired me was
convinced I would fail?

I knew I could succeed because of what I had already overcome.

Up until the age of eleven, I had a normal life. I was the fifth of six children born to loving, Irish-Catholic parents. We lived a middle-class life in the Midwest. My father, a highly educated man, worked as a psychology professor in the Chicago area.

He had always dreamed of opening a clinic for early childhood education in Southern California. He had visited the San Diego area after World War II and loved everything about California. He truly believed our family could have a better life in Southern California.

Ultimately, he decided to take a leap of faith and go for his dream. He quit his job, borrowed against his teacher's pension, and moved our family to the West Coast. He took a job selling cars so he could earn money while he waited for his California teaching certificate to arrive. Once it arrived, he would be allowed to open his clinic.

It wasn't to be.

Six months after we moved to California, my father collapsed. He died of a massive heart attack on Valentine's Day, in front of my mother, my siblings, and me. He was fifty years old. I was only eleven.

In an instant, our lives changed forever. My father left our family a $10,000 life insurance policy. That was it. He never imagined that he wouldn't be there to provide for the family he cherished. Since he had borrowed against his teacher's pension, there was no pension benefit available for our family. We went from middle class to broke, overnight.

From that day forward, everyone in our family had to work. My mother needed all of us to pull our weight financially just to keep the lights on. I got my first job before I turned twelve. I earned $1 per hour as a babysitter. I was lucky; most of my friends were working for fifty cents an hour! Every dime my siblings and I made had to be turned over to our mother so she could keep a roof over our heads and food on the table. Her only income was her Social Security benefit. She received $88 per month for me and my sister, and a small benefit for herself. That was it. I remember my mother pulling me aside and telling me point blank, "If you ever want to get out of poverty, you are going to have to do it on your own. I can't help you." From a young age, I learned both the power and necessity of a strong work ethic.

We were barely scraping by when tragedy struck again. I was sixteen years old, driving to my first "real" job at McDonald's, when I was involved in a terrible accident with a motorcyclist. The driver of the motorcycle was killed, and I was charged with involuntary manslaughter. My mother and I met with an attorney. She was honest about our family's financial situation.

After hearing our story, the attorney spoke to my mother as if I wasn't even there. "Mrs. McGowan," he said, "this is purely a matter of economics. If your daughter pleads guilty to these charges, I will be happy to enter the plea at no cost to you. Your daughter will get the appropriate sentence prescribed by the State of California. But, if she wants to defend herself, it will cost you a lot of money."

I thought surely Mother would never agree to that. I was wrong.

My mother took a minute to consider what he had said. Then the next thing I knew, I heard her thank him and acknowledge we had no other option. She told him I would plead guilty!

I was *horrified*. I begged and pleaded with my mother. That's when she looked at me and said the ten words I will never forget:

"Honey, we have no money; therefore, we have no choice."

That was the day I learned *money buys you choices*.

Fortunately, not long afterward, another option presented itself. My older brother had just begun his real estate career and suggested we take out a second mortgage on our home to pay for my defense. We did so, and with the money from the mortgage, our attorney was able to bring in expert witnesses who proved that the motorcyclist was driving well over the speed limit and that he had hit me, not the other way around.

The judge dropped all charges. At the end of the court proceeding, he said, "Take this little girl home. She's been through enough."

I wish the story ended there, but it didn't. Shortly after the criminal proceeding, the family of the young motorcyclist sued my mother and me for a substantial sum of money. I was shocked when the civil suit papers came in the mail because the man's parents had visited me at our home soon after the accident and personally assured me they would not sue me. They told me not to worry; they knew a lawsuit wouldn't bring back their son. So when the lawsuit appeared, I was devastated. Still a young girl, I had hoped my life could go back to normal but that wasn't to be.

I went through more depositions, more lines of questioning. It seemed my life would never be normal again.

My mother was terrified that we would lose the only asset she possessed, our family home. She lived with this fear for many years until the case was finally settled, at the eleventh hour, by our auto insurance company, which had come to my defense.

• • •

These early experiences taught me a lot about the power of money. I learned that without money as a resource, you were basically helpless and could easily be victimized by the system. I learned that the legal system is a scary place, especially for a sixteen-year-old. No one cared that it was an "accident"; they were looking to assign blame. I learned who my true friends were. It's amazing who you can count on when the chips are down. They are usually few and far between.

After the accident, I became what can only be called a workaholic. I held several jobs so I could earn enough to pay back my mother's second mortgage and put aside money for college. I realized the only way I was going to get out of poverty was to work hard and get a good education.

I got lucky and received a full scholarship (for all four years) to the University of California, Irvine. I even tried to "rush" a sorority but found it so ridiculous. There I was with all these carefree freshman girls who were holding candles and singing songs and next to them, I felt like a forty-five-year-old woman. I had gone through so much. I couldn't relate to any of them.

I ended up quitting the first semester. Much to the dismay of many of my friends' parents, I went home and went to work.

My mother never tried to convince me to stay at UC-Irvine. I had told her I wanted to quit and got no argument from her. In truth, even though my father was highly educated, my mother found no value in education. After all, her highly educated husband had left her destitute. But she did make me enroll in junior college as a full-time student. If I didn't, she would lose her $88 a month Social Security benefit. She made it clear that wasn't an option.

So, I went to junior college full time and worked full time. I stocked grocery shelves from 4:00 a.m. to 11:00 a.m. and then went to school. Sometimes I worked the graveyard shift, and sometimes I worked double shifts and took classes on the weekends. You name it; I did it.

This, ultimately, is what gave me my edge. Given my circumstances, I had no choice but to adopt a strong work ethic, acquire a strong set of coping skills, and demonstrate the resilience to overcome anything that was thrown my way. I often tell people I am either like the "Energizer Bunny" or one of those dolls that gets knocked over and bounces right back up.

· · ·

One really good thing happened as a result of the car accident—a schoolmate I found attractive finally noticed me.

A few months before the accident, on the first day of algebra class, as roll call was being taken, I noticed a great-looking boy named Bob Botsford sitting at the front of the class. He was the most gorgeous human being I had ever seen. Right then and there, I told my two best friends that one day I was going to marry him! Unfortunately, he didn't notice me whatsoever until the Sunday after my car accident. That day, he opened our local newspaper and saw my picture and the story of the accident on the front page! He told his parents, "That girl is in my algebra class."

Needless to say, once the accident occurred, my life and my priorities changed. I had to grow up overnight, not willingly but out of necessity. I was no longer the girl on the drill team and class council who laughed a lot. I was the talk of the town. Everywhere I went, I heard the whispers of people saying, "There's that girl that killed that boy."

I had no time to think about Bob Botsford or anyone else. I was too busy giving depositions—a process that lasted for years—plus working full time and going to school. Lucky for me, Bob pursued me, and we started dating during all this chaos. God love him; he definitely stood by me during some pretty horrible moments.

I had another fortuitous thing happen as well. I got to be a contestant on *Wheel of Fortune*, and I won (ironically winning by solving the puzzle "Down in the Dumps")!

People often ask me, "With everything going on in your life, how did you end up on the *Wheel of Fortune*?" That's an easy answer. When I turned nineteen, Bob asked me to marry him. The bride's parents are supposed to pay for the wedding. Of course, my family had no money to pay for a wedding, so I had to figure out a way to pay for it myself. In the meantime, my friend, Marie, mentioned *Wheel of Fortune* was doing tryouts for "Brides Week" in Burbank. I went to Burbank, tried out, got on, and won!

Thanks to my winnings, and my diligence at saving most of what I had earned, I had accumulated a nest egg of about $22,000—which was no small sum in 1979.

A few months before I married Bob, I invested $3,000 to buy a townhouse in San Diego County with a friend of mine. I was twenty and he was nineteen. We each invested $3,000 and obtained a mortgage for the rest. We rented it for a total of fourteen years and sold it for a decent profit. I decided through that experience I was probably not cut out to be a landlord. After each tenant moved out or was evicted, we had to re-paint and often re-carpet. It certainly cut into our profits.

Soon after Bob and I married, we entrusted the balance of our savings ($19,000) to a stockbroker, who had convinced us we were being smart by investing our "wealth" for future growth. He put our money in four different investments. In hindsight, none of them were appropriate for us. All four investments went belly-up in a very short period of time, and we lost every cent we had entrusted to him.

I was devastated. While it may not have been much money to our broker, it was everything to us! It represented years and years of hard work and sacrifice. I felt stupid, betrayed, and embarrassed. From that day forward, I made it my mission to learn everything I could about money and investing. I was determined never to let what happened to me happen to anyone I cared about.

That experience taught me some valuable lessons that have helped me in my career as a financial advisor. As a result, I really understand, from the client's perspective, how scary it must feel to turn your money over to an advisor, often a stranger, and "hope for the best." I know what it feels like to wake up one day and be surprised that all your life savings are gone . . . poof! I think the worst part of the experience was that our broker just shrugged it off. He never apologized because he really didn't care.

Here is the lesson from this:

Don't touch other people's money unless you genuinely care what happens to it.

Obviously, all these experiences shaped the way I feel about money and investing. They gave me the impetus to find my way to this profession. I was able to see up close what poor financial planning—or worse yet, NO financial planning—can do to a family. I know from firsthand experience how easily I could have landed in jail, despite the fact that I had committed no crime, simply because my family didn't have the money to pay for a lawyer. I often wonder how that scenario would have played out; I shudder to think about it. I also learned that accidents happen in an instant. No one gets in their car thinking they will hurt someone that day. I've learned that without good financial planning, an accident that results in a civil lawsuit can threaten to take away everything you have worked so hard to achieve.

I also learned that life happens. Accidents happen. Stock markets happen. Markets go up. Markets go down. I've experienced so much, and like you, I have dedicated the better part of my life to helping people find their way through the countless minefields that threaten to take away their ability to enjoy the fruits of their labor.

• • •

Finally, one of the most important lessons I learned is that clients don't want to work with glitzy salespeople in fancy suits with silk ties who show them canned pitch decks or marketing slicks or Callan charts. They want someone who is real and transparent on a personal level. While clients want you to listen to them, they also want to know your story and hear about struggles you have had to overcome.

Every person alive has had challenges, and the financial advisor who can best relate to those challenges has the advantage. For those of you who have led relatively "charmed lives" with few personal challenges, don't think you have nothing to offer here. The stories don't have to be yours. They can be borrowed. You don't have to have similar things happen to YOU to be able to relate to a client. But you must have stories about people you know or have worked with to be able to relate. It's in the relating where all the magic occurs.

MY PROFESSIONAL STORY

From age eleven to twenty-two, life was certainly tough for me. I had no idea then that I would end up with a fabulous business that allowed me to help many people and create a great life for myself and my family. After all I had been through, it was inconceivable to me that life would be anything but difficult and painful; that's all I had ever known.

Fortunately, things did turn around. However, I have to say that nothing has ever come easy for me. I have had to work exceptionally hard for everything I have. And that's why my early circumstances, as tough as they were, were a blessing. They gave me the confidence to know I can overcome all obstacles.

PRE-FINANCIAL SERVICES
INDUSTRY EXPERIENCE

After my husband, Bob, graduated from San Diego State University, he became a US Air Force officer, and we set out on our journey to see the world. The requirements of training to be an F-15 fighter pilot are quite arduous, so as I said earlier, we moved seventeen times in the first fourteen years we were married. It was a wonderful adventure, and I loved every move and every new opportunity, even though it did require me to start over in a new college every time.

During this period, I was lucky to get jobs in the real estate area, specifically as a title insurance officer. I also took college classes at night. It took me eleven years and seven colleges, but I finally graduated summa cum laude from the University of Maryland, European division.

My first entrepreneurial adventure started when we were stationed in Bitburg, Germany. There were no job opportunities in Germany for military wives like me, so we had to find jobs on the air base, which were few and far between.

Fortunately, my knowledge of real estate came to my rescue. In fact, I found myself counseling friends who were getting ready to return to the United States. In those days, (1985–1988) everyone returning home wanted to buy a house. So, I would sit down with my friends and share ideas on how to go back to the States and use their veteran's benefits to buy a home with no money down. I realized I was somewhat of an expert on that subject.

One day a friend of mine, who noticed I was counseling friends and scribbling down ideas on the back of a cocktail napkin, suggested I go to the base education office and offer to teach a formal class on the subject. Keep in mind, I had never taught anything to anyone, nor did I feel comfortable speaking in public. However, I was bored and thought this might be a good challenge; after all, I certainly knew a lot about the subject matter. So, I went into the office of Morale, Welfare, and Recreation (MWR) and asked if I could teach a real estate class.

The woman who ran the office fired off her very first question: "How much are you going to charge for the class?"

"Oh, I wasn't planning to charge anything," I replied. "I am just a housewife looking for something to do."

And then the woman said something profound:

"Well, if you don't charge anything for the class, no one will come. People value what they pay for."

Aha!

People value what they pay for.

What an amazing lesson and a truism that has stuck with me to this day.

I finally blurted out I would charge $25 per person (mind you, this was going to be for an eight-hour class). I would get to keep $20 per person, and the other $5 went to MWR for advertising, etc.

She was fine with that. She also told me that if I were smart, I would create flyers and get a high school student or an enlisted person to post my flyers in the stairwells of apartments on the base, at the base grocery store, in the community bank, and at any other place frequented by most people on base.

She ended our conversation by telling me she would put my class in the semester catalog. I had so little confidence in myself that I just assumed my class would be put in the catalog somewhere between cake decorating and dog obedience!

I quickly went into action, creating my materials for the class. This was 1986, so there was no such thing as PowerPoint. I typed up my syllabus and notes and copied them to transparencies because I planned to use an overhead projector. Then I set about creating flyers. Wow, before I knew it, I was learning how to market myself! I had never done that before.

To make a long story short, I gave my first real estate seminar on January 25, 1987, to twenty-two people. I had never stood up in front of people or spoken in public before. I can't say I was terrified, but I did feel a lot of apprehension. My saving grace? I knew my topic cold. I had closed hundreds and hundreds of loans in my career so there was little chance my audience would be able to ask me a question I didn't know how to answer.

That was just the start. In the years that followed, I was invited to speak at many, many military bases throughout central Europe. My classes were a big hit. In fact, the newspaper, *Air Force Times*, did a full-page story on my classes, and I was given the opportunity to appear on Armed Forces Television. I was a TV star!

The entire experience of teaching those classes laid the foundation for what was to come. Each experience in my life somehow prepared me for a future assignment. Hence, I never consider anything "random." It has all been a part of the tapestry of my life.

ENTERING THE FINANCIAL SERVICES PROFESSION

We returned to the United States in October 1988. My first thought was to return to the title insurance business or work in real estate. I was offered a job as a mortgage broker and thought that was where I would end up.

However, the Sunday before I was to begin work, we were in church when a lady was paged and had to leave the service. I figured she was a doctor or something similar to that. When I found out she was a mortgage broker, I knew I didn't want the job. I did not want to work in a business where I would be at the whims of others to the extent that I would have to leave church on Sunday or work on weekends. I know that sounds superficial, but I was determined to have balance in my work and personal life. After all, I had a husband and a son.

Once I made that decision, I had no idea what I was going to do. Fortunately, a friend of mine told me about her stockbroker, Hal Burleson, and said she thought she could get me an appointment with him. I did not own a business suit or a briefcase, so when the appointment was set, I had to borrow a suit and briefcase from a friend.

I met with Hal, and he explained in detail what it was like being a stockbroker. Truthfully, I didn't know a stock from a bond and could barely spell mutual fund, but when he said he could probably get me an interview with the branch manager, I was very excited.

On the day of my first interview to become a stockbroker, I was both excited and apprehensive. I was convinced this man was going to recommend that I become someone's secretary. Instead, he said, "Well, kid, I'm going to give you a chance, and I'm going to hire you!" I couldn't believe it. Someone took me seriously! (Or so I thought at the time . . .)

I started studying for the Series 7 test in March 1989, and passed all my tests and trainings by July 1989.

After spending three weeks training at the home office, I came back and was ready to begin my new career. And that's when I had that fateful meeting, I described in the introduction. In case you skipped over the introduction (as I often do), let me recap it here.

That was the day I presented my prospective business plan to my new boss.

I had worked *very* hard on it. I wanted to bowl him over and get my career off to a good start.

He *was* impressed with my business plan and said: "Honey, I have to give you a lot of credit. You have come up with an incredible business plan, probably better than most I have seen."

It's what he said next that stopped me in my tracks.

"I have to tell you up front—and I don't want you to be disappointed, but this is never going to work," he said. "You are a sure recipe for disaster." I was stunned and when I asked him why he thought that he said plainly: "Because you are young, you are a female, and this is the South. It's never going to work."

I don't remember how that meeting ended, but I look back and often think those were the kindest words he could have spoken. That day I determined I was going to make him eat those words. I was not going to fail—ever! The phrase "Failure is not an option" became my mantra. That mantra has probably helped me more than any thought I have ever had.

EARLY CHALLENGES BRING VALUABLE LESSONS

Starting out in Panama City, Florida, in 1989 was not easy. The average per capita income at the time was little more than $9,000 per year, and that was true for military personnel as well. We used to call the area L.A. (Lower Alabama). In addition, I didn't know one person in town outside of my husband, and he only had limited resources to invest (like nothing)! But I was determined, and I worked hard. One clear break came: My friend, Hal Burleson, quickly became my mentor. God love him; he was probably single-handedly responsible for my success, and I have probably never adequately thanked him for that. So, again, Hal, THANK YOU!

Hal had been in business two years longer than me and let me follow him around like a puppy dog. He shared every tool and trick of the trade he had learned thus far. I have to say, Hal operated from an attitude of abundance, which was unusual in those days. Most of the other brokers would lock up their desks and their offices and would never share their ideas or marketing techniques. I was fortunate that Hal shared everything he learned. I was a sponge for everything I could absorb. Hal was using public seminars to build his business, and he was kind enough to let me come be his "assistant" so I could learn his techniques. He even went so far as to let me copy, verbatim, his seminar materials!

Hal believed there was more than enough business to go around, even in a small town like Panama City, so he freely shared what he was doing with me. It was an unbelievable gift. Along with the seminars, Hal and I started working on some other marketing endeavors as a part of the multifaceted marketing "machine" we were working on at the time. By the end of my first year in business, Hal came to me and said, "Erin, I have never seen a more determined business person in my entire life—male or female. I can't believe how driven you are." Hal was right; I was driven. As I was to discover later, I was driven by the fear of failure. I knew what poverty looked like, and I knew I was never going back there.

Three Major Lessons I Learned During This Time

- Starvation is a wonderful motivator.

- It is better to operate from an attitude of abundance than an attitude of scarcity; there is enough business to go around for everyone.

- Always err on the side of generosity. Hal would drop whatever he was doing when I entered his doorway. He would put down his pen and focus on my question. He was incredibly generous with his time.

A CHANCE ENCOUNTER CHANGED IT ALL

I wish I could say those early lessons were the ultimate keys that unlocked my success, but I'd be lying. Only three and a half years into my career, my husband decided to get out of the US Air Force and move to Dallas, Texas, to become an airline pilot with American Airlines. My marriage being a priority, I knew I had no choice but to move and once again, I started over. I moved a good bit of my book of business but starting over is never easy; it feels like walking through a foot of mud as you figure out the landscape. Lo and behold, about a year after arriving in Dallas, another broker in my office came up to me with a proposition. He was a penny stock trader and one of his clients was the head of Human Resources for a large electronics firm. They were offering an "early out" to nine hundred of their employees. This broker said: "I hear you're the seminar queen. How would you like to get in front of nine hundred people being offered early retirement?" Of course, it seemed like a dream come true. Also, of course, this guy said he wanted fifty percent of any revenue from that opportunity. Truth be told, I thought he would do half of the work but instead, he took off for Mexico, leaving me to sink or swim on my own efforts. The branch manager provided no help either.

Over the next couple of weeks, I did three seminars with three

hundred people in each room. After each seminar, there were people lined up around the room to schedule a meeting with me. It
was thrilling and yet overwhelming. The only help I had was a
part-time assistant I shared with four other brokers, so I enlisted
the help of my husband. These were not large accounts but there
were a lot of them. I would call my assistant and say: "They have
$400,000; give them plan A" or call my husband and say: "They
have $700,000; give them plan B." It was all I could do to keep up.

I remember waking up on December 23rd of that year so
exhausted. I hadn't slept in days; I hadn't bought a tree for
Christmas, and I didn't have one present for my son. It was a true
awakening for me as I asked myself: "Is it worth it?" Eventually, as
you'll hear, I decided it wasn't.

The sad thing about this entire story is that it could have been
a dream come true, but I didn't have the resources to capitalize on
the opportunity. My branch manager should have lined up people
to help me, but he didn't. The guy who brought the opportunity
should have stayed around, but he didn't. The irony was that I
brought in over $25 million in a three-month period, which by
anyone's definition was a success, but it turned out the company
paid out $792 million!

Think about that: I had the implied endorsement of the company, but I didn't have the infrastructure or resources to capitalize
on it. I was exhausted and I wanted out. I told my husband I just
wanted to go get a job.

The next day, I went to my branch manager and told him I
was quitting. It just wasn't worth it. And bless his heart . . . even
though he was a veteran advisor, he had no clue how to help me.

Instead, he said: "Erin, come on, you're not a quitter. Just give it one more year." He also encouraged me to go find some business coaching. So, not being a quitter by nature, I decided to enroll in a coaching program, and I decided to give it one more shot.

Along the way something happened that would forever change my life. It was the third year of coaching . . . . The twelfth session. I'll never forget it as long as I live. Our coach asked us to stand up and find someone in class to review the results we'd gotten in our business over the previous three years . . . . I stood up and looked around and saw this random guy standing there and I asked him if he wanted to do the exercise together. He said yes. His name was Paul. I was so excited about my progress, I decided to go first. I told him I was from Dallas, Texas, and three years ago, before I started in this coaching program, I was doing around $300,000 in personal production. This year, three years later, I was on target to do somewhere between $400,000 and $450,000 and I was like, "Whoo hoo, look at me."

Then it was Paul's turn. He said he was from Virginia and three years earlier he had also been doing around $300,000 in production. And I started thinking: "Well, look at that; we're just alike." And then Paul said the words I will never forget. He said: "This year I'm on target to do $3 million in production . . . and I don't meet with any existing clients anymore. I've hired a team to meet with existing clients for their reviews.

"Now, my only job is to prospect for new clients, share the philosophy of our firm, and then turn them over to my team . . ." And then his voice just started trailing off . . . . Actually, it was my head that started wandering off . . . started thinking: "What did he just say? Did I miss a coaching session? Or did he go to another coaching program on Mars? I just couldn't imagine how he did that."

So, I said, "Did you just say you went from $300,000 to $3 million in three years?" To which he said, "Yep." "And you don't meet with all your clients for their quarterly reviews?" I asked. And he responded, "No, I've built an entire team around me to do that . . . ."

And I'm thinking: "How in the world did he do that?" I mean, seriously, I never knew this was even possible. Did you? Have you ever heard of a thousand percent growth in three years?

And, of course, the bell rang, and it was time to go back to our seats. I just stood there—it felt like that ALS Ice Bucket Challenge moment. It was like someone had just poured a big bucket of ice-cold water on me. I was simply dumbfounded. I started stuttering and stammering and said: "Paul, could I just buy a few hours of your time?" Lucky for me he said: "Sure, in fact, why don't you come spend the day with me and my team?"

As quickly as I could get back to Dallas, I actually made my husband come with me to his office because I just knew there was going to be a big cost to getting results like that . . . like I was probably going to have to divorce my husband (and I wanted him to understand why) and I was probably going to have to give up my firstborn child. I mean there must be some great sacrifice to get those kinds of results, right?

But it wasn't like that at all. In fact, spending one day with Paul changed everything in my business and in my life, and all for the better.

What were those results? Well, just a few short years later, I too did $3 million in production . . . and then $4 million and then $5 million and my business kept growing from there. I ended up with two offices—one in Dallas and one in Atlanta. I had seven conference rooms consistently filled with clients of my firm and I wasn't in any one of them. I had eighteen employees who worked for me and essentially ran all aspects of my business. In fact, in 2015 I took six months off, just to prove to myself that my business could run without me, and we ended up having a record year that year.

After meeting all my business goals, I sold my firm in October 2017 and decided I wanted to give back to the industry that allowed me to become so successful. I wanted to encapsulate what worked in the business and what didn't work. I wanted to help advisors avoid so many of the pitfalls I ran into along the way, so they didn't have to make all of the same mistakes I made. Essentially, I wanted to provide them with an exact blueprint for success—a detailed road map to follow so they didn't make any wrong turns toward their journey to success.

I created a training program where I teach advisors everything I learned along the way *in the shortest time possible* so they can build the businesses of their dreams. Like I modeled Paul in every area of my business, these advisors have decided to model my success and are able to significantly shorten their learning curve. The program is called the Elite Advisor Success System™ and you can find out more about it if you go to: www.erinbotsford.com.

The rest of this book are the lessons I learned along the way and the concepts I teach my advisor students.

QUESTIONS TO PONDER:

- **What has your business journey been like? Can you connect the dots to what you experienced growing up and how you were attracted to this business?**

One thing I teach my advisor students is to create a Founder's Video to allow your prospects to see you as a human. Your story needs to show that you've experienced a few setbacks or adversity along the way, but you have also overcome those challenges. Why? Because overcoming adversity is both appreciated and applauded. Do you have a Founder's Video to connect with your prospects?

- **As an advisor, do you have a success road map to follow? Is it working?**

Our business is unique in that we don't go to work for a firm and work our way up the ladder, learning as we go. Instead, we pass a few tests, hang a shingle, and are kind of left on our own with minimal business training. We are then left to figure it all out on our own. Have you ever felt frustrated that there is seemingly no road map to success in the financial services business?

- **Do you have a business or do you have a job with a great boss—YOU?**

Most businesses hire other people to do the actual work of the business. For whatever reason, that tradition has not made its way to our industry. Instead, our industry is made up of "rugged individualists" who are constantly making things up and reinventing the wheel. In addition, many advisors are resistant to the idea of replacing themselves in the room. As you'll hear time and time again in this book, if the business depends upon you to meet with every single client, it will have very little value when you are ready for an exit.

CHAPTER 2

SUCCESS BEGINS
IN YOUR MIND

Every advisor I meet wants to know the "keys to success" and I'm always happy to give them my perspective. After all, hindsight has its benefits and I've been able to look back and identify the specific key elements that led to my success.

Without a doubt, the place everyone needs to start is establishing a **Mindset of Achievement**. We all know every decision you make in any area of your life is established in your head long before you take action.

There's an old saying that came from Napoleon Hill that says: "Whatever a man can conceive and believe, he can achieve." In my case, on my way home from my day with Paul, I decided to believe I could be a top producer long before the results ever manifested themselves. I learned your brain has to stay consistent with itself. Once I decided I wanted to become a multi-million-dollar producer, then I had to find the tools, skills, and resources to make that happen.

In your case, you can make that same decision as you read these words. You can decide to become a multi-million-dollar producer and take as much time off as you choose. You just have to make that decision, internalize it, and the tools and resources will find their way to you.

Think about this: Most advisors don't think their mindset matters much. But the fact is your current mindset and your current set of skills got you where you are today. If you want a different outcome next year, something is going to have to change.

To me, if you cannot get clarity on what's going on in your head, it is virtually impossible to change your behaviors and ultimately change the results you are getting.

There were three primary "aha" moments that came to me from my one day with Paul and hopefully you'll be able to relate:

1. **I realized I was thinking WAY too small**—I needed a complete shift in my mindset. I needed to start thinking and acting like a business owner. In our time together, Paul asked me questions like: "Erin, when was the last time you saw the owner of a McDonald's franchise flipping burgers in the back? Or when was the last time the CEO of UPS delivered your package?" To both questions, the answer was "never." Real business owners hire people to do the actual work of the business. Hmm . . . I realized I really didn't have a business. I had a job with a nice boss . . . me.

2. **I realized revenue and the growth of my business would always be a problem until and unless I mastered the art of prospecting**—not just for any client but for my ideal client. Believe it or not, up until that point, I had never really

sat down and wrote out what my ideal client looked like. I just took whatever clients I managed to get in front of. If they could fog a mirror, I presumed they were qualified to be a client of mine. Another error was that I really thought if I took on a client, they would refer me to someone who had more money than they did. Experience told me this NEVER happens.

3. **I realized both skills and confidence** were going to be a problem for me so the day after I came home from Paul's office, I reached out to a local estate planning attorney and paid her to come once a week for a YEAR and train me and my assistant on everything we needed to know about estate planning, risk management, and liability planning . . . all the issues that affect high net worth people. I wanted to be prepared for the chance I got in front of one of my ideal clients.

Notice, I did the work with the expectation it would pay off, not the other way around.

Today, when people ask me how I went from failing to *Barron's* Top 100 success, I tell them: "I invested in myself, in my education, and in my future. And trust me when I tell you it paid off. But, what about you? If you had the exact success blueprint to copy or model, imagine what you could build."

These days, that is what I teach my advisor students. What's been interesting to realize is there is so much truth to that old saying: When the student is ready, the teacher will appear. Well, I'm here to tell you, "When the advisor is ready, the high-net-worth prospects will appear." When you acquire the appropriate skills, you will be able to close them in the first meeting. I'm proud to say well more than a thousand advisors have chosen to model what I said and what I did to close high net worth prospects in the first meeting. It's not rocket science, but there is a lot of science and even more psychology at play.

I also believe there is a second half to mindset and that is thinking like a business owner. To do that, I have an exercise I ask all my advisors to go through in their heads. I ask them to take a step back, pretend they are on a mountaintop or up in an airplane, and get a 30,000-foot view of their business. Then, I ask one question:

What do you want to happen on the last day you work in this business? In other words, what's your end game?

Do you plan to one day sell your business and get a big check like I did? Do you want to leave the business to your son or daughter? What exactly does that last day look like for you? You need to be able to visualize that last day. I'm here to tell you that top producers think a lot about their end game.

What I've learned is that what happens to you on that last day is going to be totally dependent upon what your business looks like on that day.

If your business depends upon you to meet with every single client, then it will have very little value in the marketplace.

Nobody will pay you top dollar for your business and risk clients walking away.

Case in point, I sold my firm in October 2017. On the same day I sold my firm, the buyer of my firm bought another woman's business. She had about the same AUM as me and about the same number of clients, but she had two big things going against her.

First, all her clients were used to meeting with her for their review meetings. Even though she had a decent-sized team, she did most of the reviews. And second, unfortunately for her, she had had a massive stroke and had to sell. Because the buyer knew her clients were dependent on her, I'm told she ended up getting twenty-five cents on the dollar compared to me.

I can't think of a worse outcome, and I don't want that outcome for any advisor who works with me. The good news is that less than an optimal outcome is totally avoidable, but it doesn't happen by chance.

I encourage you to take some time and decide what you want your end game to look like. This is such an overlooked key and yet, it's the most important place to start. If you've never really done this seriously, I want to encourage you to make it a priority.

You're good at planning for others; let's make sure you plan for yourself. For more information and additional resources, go to www.erinbotsford.com.

QUESTIONS TO PONDER:

- **What are your limiting beliefs and what changes are you going to make to eliminate them from your psyche?**

We all have limiting beliefs that determine our outcomes. When it comes to your business, what stories have you told yourself that have impacted your ability to achieve at the highest level? Have you told yourself that your humble beginnings keep you from achieving? How about the town where you live? My mentor, Amy Leavitt, was charging $14,000 per year as her minimum financial planning fee back in 1997 in the small town of Quechee, Vermont. She was able to do that because she refused to accept limiting beliefs as truth.

- **If you knew you could not fail, what changes would you make in your business and your life?**

You know that old acronym—FEAR—which is really "false evidence appearing real." Most of us allow fear to hold us back. In the end, it's the acquisition of new skills that will bring you the confidence you need to overcome any fears you may have about growing your business to any level you choose.

- **What do you want to have happen on the last day you are in business?**

  Will the current state of your business provide that outcome? If not, what changes do you need to make to ensure the outcome you desire? Remember: If your business depends on you meeting with every client, it will have very little value in the marketplace.

- **Are you thinking way too small when it comes to your business goals?**

  My one day with Paul was a game changer. I realized I was thinking WAY too small. I realized I didn't have the skill set or confidence to approach and close my "ideal" clients. What about you? Are you thinking too small when it comes to your business goals? Do you have the skill set and confidence to attract your ideal prospects and close them the first time you meet with them?

CHAPTER 3

FIRST THINGS FIRST— LEARN AND MASTER THE "SECRET SAUCE"

One of the biggest questions I get from advisors is: "How do I find high net worth clients to work with?" My answer is always the same: "If I were to put you in a room full of $20 or $30 million clients, would you know how to close them? Would you know what their issues are and what their hot buttons are? Could you close them in the first meeting?" Typically, the answer is "NO."

I follow up with: "Then why would you want to get in front of high net worth prospects if you have no idea how to close them?"

The truth is it doesn't matter how good your marketing and prospecting methods are; if you don't know what to say when you get in front of a qualified prospect, it's pretty much all wasted time.

Note the word "qualified." I learned the hard way that not every person who can fog a mirror is qualified to be your client. So, the first thing every advisor needs to do is identify their "ideal" client.

Is it a small business owner, a retiree, a senior-level executive at a Fortune 500 company, a professional athlete, or a widow?

It's important to take a good bit of time to evaluate your marketplace and write down the attributes of your ideal client. For instance, if you're in a small town and have no access to professional athletes, why would you put them on your ideal client list? That said, if you have natural connections because you were a former athlete, then in this virtual world, you might be able to include that persona.

Notice the word "persona." You can have more than one ideal client. I call them "personas." In my case, I had retirees, executives at Fortune 500 companies, and small business owners. I eventually got to work with a few professional athletes but those were never on my target market list; those introductions came through a strong referral program.

The biggest reason to spend time identifying your ideal client is to eliminate wasting your time on wild goose chases where there's no chance your ideal client is going to be.

But let's assume you identify your ideal prospect and have the opportunity to get in front of them. What I learned in my career and now teach is that there are a few key elements that must happen in your first meeting with a prospect in order to close them in the first meeting.

I call this first meeting your "Approach Talk." Adopting these key elements will also help you move upmarket.

First off, at the scheduled meeting, everything needs to be perfectly staged. I had a specific greeting and seating system, which was critical to the outcome I wanted. For instance, every prospect or client had to be greeted within two minutes of their arrival. They were greeted and while they were still in the lobby, they were asked what they wanted to drink. My employee would get their preferred beverage and then place that beverage in the conference room exactly where I wanted each of the prospects to sit. This all happened before I walked into the room.

And here's a huge takeaway—in fact if you make this one little change, your closing ratio is likely to go up.

You always want to seat the woman at the head of the table and the man when he's looking at you, there should be nothing behind you to distract him.

Now, you might be asking why should you sit the woman at the head of the table? Well, there's about an encyclopedia's worth of psychology that should be discussed on this topic but the bottom line is that, in our society, there's an unspoken rule and that rule is that even if the woman is not the powerhouse breadwinner, she does have a superpower she can use at will.

I call that superpower **absolute veto power**. Most men I work with completely understand this superpower because they've been on the receiving end of this power and it's not always pleasant! Regardless, trust me when I tell you, if she feels ignored in the meeting or if she feels marginalized in any way, by the time she gets to the car and closes the door, you'll be history. So, if there's only one thing you remember about closing prospects, it should be this: Always seat the woman at the head of the table and include her in the conversation. Don't start talking football, hockey, golf, or baseball with her husband or you'll lose her even before you get started. You never want her to exercise her superpower.

A critically important part of being able to close prospects of any size is understanding some basic human psychology. It's important to recognize that people will generally not see the need for your services or financial planning in general, unless or until they have some kind of a triggering event in their life. That might be getting married, having a baby, getting divorced, losing a parent, getting a new job, retiring, etc.

Now think about this: As advisors, which one of us wants to wait around for that triggering event to actually happen? Certainly, not me! So, in essence, in my first meeting with prospects, my goal was to create one or more of those triggering events in their minds. I wanted them to clearly see the ramifications to their life if they don't anticipate what happens when those triggering events actually occur.

The way I do this is to ask them a few questions about their current planning and then I ask them probing questions about what they have or have not done in terms of planning for that triggering event. I call this line of questioning "disturbing tracts."

In a few paragraphs, I will go through an example of this technique. Keep in mind, I have twenty-two of these little paths or "disturbing tracts" I can use in any given situation to create a triggering event in my prospect's mind.

Also, and this is critical: If the prospect is part of a

couple—whether they're married or not, gay or straight—both parties in the couple need to be present when you give your approach talk. This is so important that you need to insist they both be there and don't do your approach talk with just one of them. Just reschedule the meeting. It's that important.

Why? Because psychologically men and women react differently to "triggering events." Women typically want to protect their nest egg at all costs where the man, if he's like my husband, might think: "Well, if I lost it all, as long as I have a big screen TV and a futon, I'm good." A woman will NEVER feel that way.

I had one of my students ask me about doing this virtually and yes, all this works whether you're in-person or over Zoom. It's all human psychology, which NEVER changes no matter where you live or what media you use!

Just for grins, I will tell you the story of how this worked out for one of my students. Her name is Carolyn.

Carolyn had been in the business for over twenty-five years. Her average client had around $2 million with her. Right after she enrolled in my Elite Advisor Success System™, she had the opportunity to get in front of a $30 million business owner, which was a huge opportunity for her.

She told me she binge-watched my Secret Sauce course over the weekend and memorized all my disturbing tracts so she'd be uber-prepared. When she got to the meeting, the man's wife wasn't there. She knew that was the ultimate no-no. You never give an approach talk to one person if they are part of a couple.

Fortunately, she had the wherewithal to get the wife on a Zoom call, so the wife was present as Carolyn went through her approach talk. She told me when she was finished, she held her breath. The next day, the business owner called to see if she was going to be in the office. He wanted to bring by a check for $15 million, with the other $15 million coming later in the year. And the bonus was three weeks later, Carolyn got her $40 million business partner as a client! All because she was prepared with the knowledge of what to say when she got in front of them. She wasn't "winging it." She had the script down pat.

That's how powerful my Secret Sauce and those disturbing tracts are. And, as you can imagine, Carolyn's business changed overnight. Before taking my course and learning the Secret Sauce, her average client had $1 to $3 million. Today she is getting $10 to $20 million clients. It has completely changed her business . . . and her life.

And as a little plug for my course—it's all there for the taking. You too can change your business and your life in a few short hours by going to www.erinbotsford.com.

To continue: After appropriately greeting and seating your prospects and knowing this psychology, you'll want to transition into the main part of your Approach Talk. Again, every word is important here, so I suggest you copy and memorize them.

In the first few minutes of your meeting, you'll want to get to know them and give them the time to reveal as much about themselves as they feel comfortable. Some people will be very guarded, and some will just "throw up all over you." You always hope for the latter but that doesn't always happen. The more information you can get them to reveal about themselves up front the better. You can start formulating which disturbing tracts might be most appropriate to these prospects. For instance, if you find out they have a second home on a lake, there's an amazing disturbing tract for that scenario. If you find out they have teenage drivers driving vehicles in their name, that will set up a disturbing tract. So, either write down what you hear or keep mental notes of what they have told you; you will need it in a few minutes.

Once you have gotten to know them a little and gotten as much information as they are willing to reveal, it will be time for you to talk.

You'll want to say: "I want to thank you both for meeting with me today. *You may be wondering how I got into this business and why I'm uniquely qualified to help you with your financial planning.*"

Then you'll want to tell your personal story. Why? Because this is a people business, and they want to know all about you. They are sizing you up and the number one question they are asking themselves is: "Can I trust him/her?" That's all they really want to know. The rest is just mechanics.

You'll want to alleviate the trust concerns they may have by telling your personal story. Ideally, you want to be able to tell it in three minutes or less. You want to highlight something crappy that happened to you along the way, but then demonstrate how you overcame it. This is critical but it's easy to mess up. You either end up talking too much about yourself, or you leave yourself in the mud puddle and you never overcome the challenge. One of the many reasons this is important is that people want to see you as human, they want to know you have experienced something tough in your life, they want to see that you overcame that obstacle, and that the lessons you learned have added to the tapestry of your life. The bottom line is in our culture, overcoming adversity is both appreciated and applauded so you want to give your prospects an opportunity to feel you're worthy of their trust.

In the interest of time, I eventually turned this into a "Founder's Video" and had my staff tee up the video before I ever walked into the room. It kept my story succinct and consistent. I was able to make sure all the psychological elements were included because it was scripted and professionally filmed. I encourage my advisor students to follow my exact formula for creating a Founder's Video, so it does the job it's supposed to do—garner trust.

Once I'd told my story, I'd launch into my approach talk.

In my practice, we always focused first on risk management. Why? Because clients were expecting me to start talking about the investments I used or my manager selection process. Why is that? Because that's what the last financial advisor they met with did. So, if are you looking for a way to stand out from all your competition, you'll want to pay close attention to this next section.

Again, to distinguish myself from everyone else out there, I always started around risk management. I would begin by saying: "Rather than start our discussion today talking about your investments, I'd like to begin our discussion around risk management. Why, you might ask?

"Because it's my belief that whether you have $1 million or $10 million, or anywhere in between, if an event happens . . . and let me assure you those events happen in a split second of time. If that event results in you losing all your money, then I don't really care how well your investments are positioned, it's just that much more money for you to lose."

Now, it's important to pause and step back. Did you pick up on what I just wrote? I said: "Whether you have $1 million or $10 million or anywhere in between . . . ." I said those words on purpose. The lower number I start with is what I am guessing they have. Then I ten times that number just to make a point, and that point is that I'm very used to working with people who have the amount of money they have; in fact, I'm comfortable working with people who have ten times what they have.

Keep in mind, I haven't said I work with people who have ten times what they have, but just by positioning it this way, people assume you work with people much wealthier than they are. It's interesting to see the reaction of a guy who comes in with $10 million and he thinks he's all that and you start by saying:

Whether you're worth $10 million or $100 million or anywhere in between . . . if an event happens and that event causes you to lose all your money . . . and then you just watch their reaction. It definitely sets the stage and puts you in a position of power and credibility at that moment. If you ever had a "closed off" prospect, you know what I mean. This is the best way to get them to open up and get them into a state of listening to you.

Do you see how this is all scripted out because every word is important? That's because it works!

The next step of our initial meeting with a prospect involves using those "disturbing tracts" I mentioned before. This is the single biggest success strategy that will make the greatest impact on your closing ratio. That is why I call it my "Secret Sauce" because the words I use are literally worth their weight in gold.

I have found, in order to get a prospect to give you the big YES in the first meeting, you have to expose vulnerabilities in what they have done in terms of planning for their future, and I'm talking about what they have done in the NON-investment areas of their lives. I'll say that again: You want to expose problems in the NON-investment areas of their lives. This is where it gets fun! This is how my students are able to move upmarket very quickly.

You can be pretty confident that most of your competitors have only focused on the investment and retirement side of the business. After all, that's where all the money is and it's pretty easy to do. But it's not all that effective. Why?

Because the prospect is expecting you to pull out your Callen charts or your pitch deck and start discussing your investment strategies or maybe your management selection process. So don't do that.

Instead, you want to build on your personal story and the rapport you've started to create and now you want to start disturbing them.

One of my favorite disturbing tracts is asking the prospects simple questions about the flow of inheritance to their children. I simply ask them to tell me a little bit about the provisions in their current estate plan. Specifically, I'll ask them: "Mr. and Mrs. Smith, can I assume when the first of you dies, the money goes to the survivor of the two of you?" And typically, they'll say "yes."

"Okay, then can you tell me, when the second of you dies, according to your current documents, how the money is distributed to your children?" (and notice what I say next . . .)

"Tell me, does the money flow to your children **outright or do they receive their inheritance in some form of graduated**

distribution . . . like maybe they get ⅓ of it when they turn thirty, ⅓ at age thirty-five, and the remainder at age forty. How are your current documents set up?"

And then I just wait for their answer.

Typically, they have no recollection about the provisions in their estate planning documents and they'll usually look at each other and chat for a moment. And in most cases, they'll just guess. And the good thing is that regardless of how they answer me, I have a way to respond back to them.

If they have a lot of money, they will often guess that they leave their money to their children in some form of graduated distribution, because they think it is more sophisticated than an outright distribution. So, they'll say something like: "Yes, I think it's graduated. I think they get some at thirty, some at thirty-five, and the rest of it when they turn forty."

If that ends up being their answer, I'll pause for a moment and say: "Hmmm, I find that interesting." Another pause . . . and then I'll paint a few potential scenarios for them:

"So, let's just pretend at the time of your death, your youngest son is forty-two . . . And he happens to be going through a divorce. Based on what you just told me, if your documents are set up as a graduated distribution and if you're correct, your children end up with ALL of their money at the age of forty, then at age forty-two you would have blown through all of the graduations and your son would be getting all of the money outright. Do you see that?" They will typically nod.

"And if that's the case, what if your son happens to be going through a divorce? Do you really want half the money you were going to leave to your son available to be split with your soon-to-be-ex-daughter-in-law? Is that an outcome you'd be comfortable with?"

I don't rush this dialog because I want them to see this potential outcome clearly in their minds. I want them to see the judge hitting the gavel on the table giving their soon-to-be-ex-daughter-in-law half of the money they expected to leave their son. (It's really interesting when their children are young or in their teens, but they can still visualize whom they will marry and this less-than-optimal outcome.)

I will then continue on with other worst-case scenarios like: "What if one of your children becomes a doctor and is being sued for malpractice? Or your daughter is in a car accident and is being sued for damages. Would you really want the money you leave to your children to be available to satisfy a malpractice lawsuit or a judgment of any kind?"

They will always say: "Of course not. We want the money to go to our kids and our grandkids." I will acknowledge their concerns and say: "Well, not to worry; if we work together, we can get that fixed."

Mind you, I do not tell them *how* we are going to fix those problems. They have to hire me and pay me a financial planning fee to get that done.

There are twenty-two different disturbing tracts I teach my advisor students in a complete course dedicated to mastering the appropriate use of these disturbing tracts to land a new client the first time you meet with them.

What is interesting is that I can tell I have a new client when I see the husband sweating or the wife starts punching him in the side, saying "We need to get this taken care of." It usually takes two or three disturbing tracts to get them to say "yes." It's also interesting to see the guy start sweating because he starts to see his assets as vulnerable to things other than the stock market. He's typically prepared for stock market fluctuations but not lawsuits because one of his kids gets drunk and hits someone while they're away at college. The bottom line is they have no idea how vulnerable they are and it's your job to point that out.

At this point, I want to ask you a question: "Do you see the power of proper questioning with a purpose?"

It's not to bond with them but to "disturb them" into action!

Keep in mind, the actual "Secret" to the "Secret Sauce" is this:

To win over prospects, you have to very clearly demonstrate the consequences of doing nothing— the consequences of inaction.

You want to paint a picture in their minds, first by pointing out the pitfalls that exist in the planning they have done thus far and then by illustrating the consequences to them and their families for doing nothing. If you do this correctly, the people sitting in front of you MUST make a decision. They HAVE TO FIX these problems. To do otherwise could potentially be disastrous. Think about it: Most prospects don't realize they are one car accident away from losing everything they've worked for. One accident. It's your job to point out that potential problem and get it fixed.

And by the way, discussing these pitfalls is not operating out of fear. These are legitimate issues that exist in the prospect's life that have never been addressed. It's your job as a fiduciary to address these issues. And I cannot tell you one time—not one time— where I couldn't identify something that was missing or awry in their planning.

I can also tell you if you don't get the prospect to say "yes" in the first meeting, it's because you failed to paint a picture in their heads of what could happen if they don't get these weaknesses fixed. I was able to get really good at this because I had a policy that I didn't chase prospects. If I couldn't close them in the first meeting, that was on me. I had failed to paint that picture. The next time I'd have to do better because that opportunity was gone. I can honestly say having a policy that you close prospects in the first meeting and you don't chase them afterward will ensure you'll get good at closing.

Also keep in mind, most advisors don't do any of this, so it ends up being a key differentiator for the advisor who learns all of these disturbing tracts. Most advisors never talk about the pitfalls that exist in the non-investment areas of the prospects' lives. They focus on the retirement and investment side and in the prospects' minds, it's like *blah, blah, blah* . . . . Because they think they've heard it all before.

Finally, and this should be obvious by now, but let's talk about **what NOT to do** in the first meeting. You must resist the urge to bring out your pitch deck and Callen charts, or talk about your manager selection process. Why is that? Because you don't want to sound exactly like every other financial advisor they've ever met with. So don't go there.

Typically, you'll know you have a new client when they say: "What's it going to take to get these problems fixed?" What they are really asking you is: "What's your financial planning fee?"

If you are not charging financial planning fees, you are missing out on a huge opportunity. People *want to pay for advice*. They are used to paying their CPA, estate planning attorney, doctor, dentist, massage therapist—essentially every other professional. If you do not charge a planning fee, you will not be considered credible. In fact, I'll say it is impossible to move upmarket and work with higher net worth prospects if you don't charge financial planning fees. You just won't be credible in their minds. The financial planning fee needs to be relative to their net worth. You can't charge a $30 million client a $2,500 planning fee. They will laugh you out of their office. That type of client would expect to pay at least $30,000–$50,000 annually to a professional advisor.

Case in point, one of my advisor students, Dustin, had been in the business for fifteen years and had never charged a financial planning fee. Five weeks into my program he had an opportunity to get in front of a $40 million business owner. Once again, he told me he binge-watched my Secret Sauce course and went in prepared with his disturbing tracts. At the end, the prospect said: "What's it going to take to get these issues fixed?" Dustin told me he was remembering my words, which were: "When you get in that position, say the biggest number that can possibly come out of your mouth." He told the prospect, "My annual financial planning fee is $44,500," and the prospect replied: "Done!"

My question for you is: "Do you think Dustin will ever work for free again?" When I asked Dustin that question, he said: "Not a chance."

Neither should any advisor. As a professional, our time, wisdom, and expertise are worth a lot. We can save our clients from literal disaster. What's that worth to them? I teach my students that you can give anyone an hour of your time but after that, the computer doesn't get opened up or turned on unless there's a financial planning fee check in hand.

Of course, I have very specific wording on describing the three ways you get paid. It's all just memorization and it works every time. To find out more about my course and move upmarket quickly, go to www.erinbotsford.com.

QUESTIONS TO PONDER:

- **Do you have a formalized structure and an exact process for your initial prospect meeting? What is it called? What are the repeatable steps?**

In order to be successful *every single time*, you should have a well-scripted process that will guarantee you a successful outcome with prospects.

- **Having a policy where I didn't chase prospects made me get very good at closing prospects of any size in the first meeting. Do you have that policy?**

If a prospect says "no" to you, it's imperative to diagnose, with precision, exactly what went wrong. One thing you can be sure of is that a "no" means the prospect did not walk away with a clear understanding of the consequences of inaction. That problem, while easy to diagnose, must be fixed immediately.

- **Are you leading with investments? If so, how do you distinguish yourself and your investment process from your competitors?**

Prospects are expecting you to lead with investments. If you want to differentiate yourself from every other advisor, you have to lead with something different. In my case, I led with risk management and estate planning. I believe it is what led to my success.

- **Prospects are moved into action when they are left with a clear understanding of the consequences of inaction. Are you helping clients see there are vulnerabilities and/or gaping holes in the non-investment areas of their lives?**

  Stories sell. Prospects have to see themselves in the stories. Also, remember it is the woman who is likely to be the decision maker in the room. A woman will typically want to protect her money for herself, for her children, and for her grandchildren, and she will move mountains to make that happen.

CHAPTER 4

PROSPECTING
AND MARKETING

Without clients to serve, you have no business. The only way to build a business is to get butts in seats! To do this, you have to prospect and/or market.

While there are differences between the two words ("prospecting" and "marketing"), the bottom line is you must identify your target market, locate potential customers in your target market, find ways to attract or get in front of them, and then effectively engage with them and convince them to become your clients. This is the most difficult and the most important part of any business. The extent to which you master this area of the business will be the extent to which you will be successful, and your business will grow.

I find it interesting that new entrants to our profession have little idea as to how they will spend their time. For instance, I frequently speak with young people who have decided to become financial planners. They have chosen this route for admirable reasons: They want to help people, they want to potentially own their own business, and they like the financial world.

They *think* they will spend their time doing research on stocks, funds, managers, and strategies. They look forward to designing portfolios for clients and guiding them through the financial planning process. They are usually very idealistic about how they will spend their working hours and daydream about the financial education they will glean along the way.

You can imagine the looks on their faces when I tell them that if they want to be successful in this business, they will be spending very little time doing the things they were expecting to do. Instead, if they want to be successful, they will spend most of their time prospecting, marketing, and building relationships.

The same is true for YOU. The degree to which you master the art of prospecting is the degree to which you will be successful in the business. Period. In reality, you have to do all of these things (analysis, research, etc.), but if you haven't done the work to find the clients, there is no reason for any of it.

In my case, I thought I would only have to prospect for seven years. Why seven? I don't know, but for some reason, I was convinced that after seven years, business would continue to roll in without doing any more prospecting. Wow, what a shock I had in store for me! Not only was I wrong on that, I was VERY wrong. I suppose there was a time I could have chosen to stay relatively stagnant in terms of the growth of the business, but if a business (any kind of business) isn't growing, it is dying. And there is no way to change that economic formula.

So, a critical key to success for any advisor is mastering the art of prospecting and marketing. You must become a professional prospector, hunter, or rainmaker—or whatever you choose to call it. Call it what you want, but if you can't master this role, you had better team up with someone who can, because you can never achieve high levels of success without having a regular stream of new prospects coming in the door.

For purposes of our discussion, I define *marketing* as something you do to promote your company and its services. It is usually an outbound activity and often does not require your personal involvement. We often did "marketing campaigns," where we sent e-mail blasts to clients, prospects, and centers of influence. We created marketing brochures as leave-behind items. You may use the marketing brochures offered by your home office; you may send newsletters, market updates, etc. All of those are marketing activities.

I think of *prospecting* as activities I did that actually required direct involvement, either by me or other members of my team. I called it hunting or rainmaking and I often said: "I am like a lioness. I hunt at night." What I meant by this is that I was out and about in my circle of influence on many evenings, attending functions, speaking, networking, etc., mostly for the purpose of "hunting down" new prospects. This *never* felt like work to me because I really do enjoy the people who attend these functions. I am someone who loves people, and I love hearing their stories. I am often accused of being a junkie for people's stories. That's a positive thing because people, for the most part, enjoy telling their stories. It's a win-win.

Another reason I made a point of being out and about in the

business community was to keep in front of people who could one day need our services. You know the saying: "Out of sight; out of mind." I didn't let myself be out of sight for too long. Keep in mind, I never did things I didn't want to do, nor would I work with anyone with whom I didn't have a shared set of values. Life is much too short to compromise your standards. And finally, I didn't just prospect at night. Over the years, I've prospected at all hours of the day, depending upon what made the most sense. In the next section, I'll explain the kinds of activities I did that worked particularly well for me.

METHODS OF PROSPECTING— DON'T GIVE UP

There are many ways of prospecting, and the good news is, *they all work.* All you have to do is commit to several methods that you will do simultaneously and work on those methods for at least eighteen months before you give up. You cannot decide to *try something* to see if it will work. It WILL work; you just have to give it sufficient time and effort. Certainly, along the way you, want to review what is working the best and what is not working as well as you had hoped, and modify your plan accordingly.

It is clear you have to be flexible, but the key is to not abandon anything for at least eighteen months. Remember, it normally takes seven or eight "hits" with a prospect before they actually commit to even meeting with you. That number is pretty constant; the mistake people make is giving up too soon, well before they have made contact with a prospect those seven or eight times. I would go so far as to say the number of "hits" required is probably even higher these days than it was twenty years ago, mainly due to the current economic environment.

Investors have been wounded in the past several decades, between the financial meltdown of 2008, the impact of Covid, and Madoff-type scandals. They're more wary than at any time I have seen in the past. They especially want to know if you have staying power. They want to see if you will still be in business eighteen months or two years from now before they will trust you with their money.

Speaking of prospecting, let's talk about "cold calling." During the three weeks I spent training at the home office, I was forced to cold-call. I hated it so much that I went back to my hotel room each night and cried. (Yes, I seriously cried every night!) However, I finally figured out how to rig the training system and started calling my husband and friends each night during our cold calling sessions. There was NO WAY I was going to build a business doing *that*. I had already determined that if cold calling was the only way to make it in this business, then I might as well quit right away. Keep in mind: Cold calling is still considered a very effective prospecting method. If it's working for you, God bless you; keep doing it. It just didn't work for me.

NO FRIENDS, FAMILY, OR NEIGHBORS

Second, even though my trainers taught me to focus my efforts on building a list of all my friends and family members as well as people in my direct circle of influence, I made it my policy to NOT do business with friends, family, or neighbors. Wow! How different is that?

Here were my reasons:

- One: I didn't know anyone in town, so I didn't have an immediate circle of influence. I knew my husband and a couple of other pilots in his squadron, and they clearly didn't have any money.

- Two: I knew I wasn't credible to friends and family. They knew I was new to the business, and I'm sure they wanted me to "practice" on other people. Then, too, *I* knew I was new to the business, and I didn't want to "practice" on my family and friends.

- Three: More important than all of this, when I announced that I had a policy where I wouldn't do business with friends, family, or neighbors, they suddenly rallied around me and wanted to help.

It's important to understand the psychology of this decision. Friends and family *want to help you.* They really do. They just don't want to help you, fearing it will be to their perceived detriment! If you don't make this statement overtly, everyone will think you are only visiting or reconnecting with them to get your hands into their back pocket so you can pull out their wallets. That is what they fear and that is what immediately puts a strain on your relationship.

Trust me, eventually, I ended up doing business with many, many friends and family members, but it took years before they looked at me and realized I was going to be in the business for a while. They surmised I had probably learned a few things along the way, and then they *came to me*, not the other way around. I never, ever asked a friend or family member for business, but ultimately most of them have come to me and said: "Erin, I know you have a policy for not doing business with friends, family, or neighbors, but I wanted to ask you if you'd make an exception for me." And in every case, I did make that exception, but it was a different dynamic than it would have been had I started out begging them for money. Instead, I did meet with friends, family members, and neighbors and asked them to introduce me to their contacts. Knowing my policy, they bent over backward to help introduce me to potential prospects. It was one of the best decisions I ever made, and I'm not sure why it isn't done more often.

SEMINARS WORKED FOR ME

Ultimately, my primary prospecting method turned out to be giving seminars, but in the beginning, I didn't know that's how it was going to turn out. Looking back, my training in Europe giving real estate seminars to GI's probably prepared me to become a public speaker. It is always hindsight that gives you clarity as to how the journey turns out. When you are in the moment, it takes small leaps of faith and belief in yourself that something is going to work! In the beginning, I didn't know what would work so I felt like I had to try everything and do it simultaneously. I thought the idea of giving seminars would be right up my alley, but there were two big problems I faced: What would I say to an audience when I knew very little about my subject matter, and how could I get people to attend?

INITIAL PROSPECTING METHODS

These were the initial methods I decided to use in my multifaceted marketing plan. Keep in mind, I sometimes have strange names for what I did, but if you go with it, you'll get what I mean. I want to go through these methods for people who are just getting started. My preferred method of prospecting ended up being referral prospecting and hosting various types of client events, but until you have your initial pool of clients, it's virtually impossible to do the latter. (I'll talk more about these two methods of prospecting in later chapters.)

Here were the four methods with which I started:

- "Drive-By Shootings"

- "Out-to-Lunch Bunch"

- Practice Seminars for People Who Were Not Qualified

- Real Seminars

"DRIVE-BY SHOOTINGS"

I know this title is horrible, but I would be disingenuous if I didn't tell you what I called it at the time. My friend/mentor Hal and I decided to challenge each other with this prospecting method. Three mornings a week, we'd leave our houses early and stop by small businesses. The objective of the game was to get there between 7:00 a.m. and 8:00 a.m., before the receptionist or gatekeeper got there. It was amazing how many small business owners we were able to meet. We would offer to bring in pizza during lunch and give their employees a financial seminar, which I called "The Money School." The business owner would frequently invite us back for a cup of coffee to discuss the economy, the markets, etc. It was a good way to get to know new people in town, and we generally found small business owners very receptive to our unannounced visits. Unfortunately for us, most of their investment capital was tied up in their businesses, which didn't serve our purposes all that well. In hindsight, these would have been ideal candidates for what I did toward the end of my career—full financial planning to uncover their personal and business risks. Today, I'm sure this is an approach I would take. Back then, I was a new stockbroker, and if the business owner didn't have the ability to write me a check for investment purposes, he or she was not a good candidate for my business.

On the other hand, because I needed audiences to practice on, the lunchtime seminars I did for the employees of these small businesses ended up making my efforts very worthwhile.

Deciding to use seminars to build my business was not without risk. Early on, I was very worried that someone in the audience might ask me a question I knew nothing about. This was a huge fear for me and with reason; I didn't have a clue about the financial markets. I decided I might as well practice with and look foolish in front of people who were not qualified to be my clients (although back then if they could fog a mirror, they were likely qualified)! That being said, this fear drove me to become a student of the financial markets, a skill set that has served me well.

"OUT-TO-LUNCH BUNCH"

This prospecting method will always be my favorite. As I said, when I first started, I knew no one in town, not one person. I figured out a way to work that to my benefit! (See, if you stay with me long enough you will realize I can turn any lemon into lemonade!) Shortly after I got back from home office training and had my business plan approved by my manager, I made a trip to the local Chamber of Commerce. The young woman behind the counter was very helpful and very nice. I will call her Jane Wynn. I asked Jane to lunch, and she agreed. Keep in mind, I knew up front Jane was likely not qualified to be a client of mine but since she worked for the Chamber of Commerce, I figured she knew all the "movers and shakers" in town, and I wanted to be introduced to them on a favorable basis.

We met the next week, and I explained to her that I was new in town and didn't know anyone. I asked her about things like where she got her hair cut and what she and her husband did for fun. In fact, I employed a very important technique I had learned from another friend, Dave Norczyk. The technique is based on engaging the law of reciprocity, which we all know intuitively. Essentially, when someone gives you something, you feel compelled to give them something in return. In application, the technique is to give the person you are with the gift of being able to talk about him or herself for an entire hour.

The idea is to: "Compliment and Ask Questions."

For an entire hour, I asked Jane all about herself, what she did for fun, where she shopped, etc. I kept the focus entirely on her. If she asked about me, I would answer only the question she asked and then I immediately went back to her. I wanted to know all about her job, how long she'd been there, and what she liked best—all very positive stuff. At the end of the lunch (which I bought), I said, "Jane, this has been so much fun for me. If you were me and you wanted to meet all the movers and shakers in Panama City, who would you meet with?" Without giving it any thought, she gave me two or three names and descriptions of what they did. She said: "For sure, you need to meet Bob the banker, Joe the attorney, and Tom, the CEO of XYZ."

I then asked if she would be willing to introduce me.

"Of course," she said.

She said she had enjoyed our lunch very much and would be more than happy to introduce me. Think about this: When was the last time anyone took an interest in YOU? When was the last time you got to talk all about yourself for an entire hour? I doubt it's ever happened. In practice, I have found taking a true and abiding interest in another person will pay dividends for years to come.

When I got back to the office, I thanked Jane for lunch with an e-mail that said something along these lines:

Jane,

It was a pleasure having lunch with you today. Thank you so much for taking time out of your busy schedule to meet with me. I learned so much about you and the city. If I can ever do anything to help you in terms of financial planning, please don't hesitate to give me a call. If you don't mind, I will keep you

on my mailing list and make sure you get invited to
my upcoming seminars. I think you'd enjoy learning
about the financial markets from my point of view.
You mentioned you thought I should meet Bob the
Banker, Joe the attorney, and Tom the CEO. I look
forward to those introductions.

To make things easier for you, my thought was to
just have you say:

Bob, I had lunch today with Erin Botsford. I
think you would benefit from getting to know her.
I'm copying Erin on this e-mail so she can follow up
with you.

Hope that makes things easy for you.

With warm regards,
Erin

Once she made the introduction, I would reply all and just say: "Thanks, Jane. Bob, I had a delightful lunch with your friend, Jane Wynn. She said you're someone I need to meet. Can I buy you lunch next week?" In at least ninety percent of the cases, the answer was "yes."

From that point forward, I had lunch meetings just like this several days a week for years and years and years. Each time I walked away with a new friend who had been given the gift of talking about themselves for at least an hour, so they always felt like the conversation was great! I built a very impressive list of people, many of whom eventually became my clients. It was probably the most fun and certainly one of the easiest methods of prospecting. The time we spent was primarily focused on them, and I felt confident they would consider reaching out to me if they needed a second opinion or a new advisor. It turned out to be true; many of those people ended up becoming clients over the years. In fact, what I figured was there was NO downside to this prospecting method. If they weren't qualified themselves, they typically had access to people who were. Sometimes they were members of clubs or organizations who had monthly meetings with outside speakers, so I asked to be introduced to the person who scheduled speakers. One time the person was the business writer for a very famous newspaper. After having lunch with her one time, with the focus entirely on her (she never once asked me a question about me) she really said: "Erin, I think this has been one of the most interesting lunch meetings I've ever had. I'd love to write a story in the business section about you." And that's exactly what happened. That article alone catapulted my business in Dallas. All that to say there are multiple benefits and outcomes by taking a true and abiding interest in another human being.

PRACTICE SEMINARS

As I mentioned earlier, I had decided to build my business by giving investment seminars, but I had no confidence in my ability to answer questions. I remember Hal reminding me that I probably knew more than ninety-nine percent of the people attending my seminars. But I needed the practice; I needed to be able to speak fluidly and know my material without stumbling, looking at notes, etc. So, I offered to give seminars almost anywhere and to anyone who would listen.

To my surprise, I found that I loved talking to firemen! I went to all the local fire stations and offered to give the firemen my seminar. Think about it: These guys were basically captive audiences. They were on duty for twenty-four hours, and unless the alarm went off, they weren't going anywhere. Besides that, they were amazing cooks! They would prepare lunch as they did each day and then I would give them my investment seminar. I did this for quite a few fire stations throughout Panama City. While very few firemen became clients, I learned plenty. They were all very intelligent and asked very good questions. They also had friends, family members, and neighbors who had money, so it worked out well for me. I would put them on my mailing list for my evening seminars, and they would invite their friends. Many of them became good referral sources for me.

Also, one very lucrative opportunity came up when I was given the opportunity to manage a portion of their pension fund. Their fund had very strict criteria on the types of investments it could hold, but I found the perfect opportunity for them. I began trading US government zero coupon bonds when the timing on bonds was perfect for this type of activity. Within the first year, we had made so much money using this strategy in a declining interest rate environment that I was asked to give a report to the board of trustees for the pension fund. The trustees had never seen their funds go up so much in such a short period of time. While I was nervous presenting to the board of trustees, it was quite an honor, and subsequently several of the trustees became my clients!

I also gave "practice seminars" in front of Sunday school classes, senior citizen groups, etc. You name it; I did it. After all, I was hungry, and as I have said before, starvation is a wonderful motivator.

REAL SEMINARS—HOW TO FILL A ROOM

Within a very short time, I went to my manager and told him I was ready for the big leagues. I wanted to start giving investment seminars, either in the evenings or during the day at public libraries. In my naiveté, I assumed my manager would pay for ads in the local newspaper, and hundreds of people would show up! Boy, was I wrong on all counts.

When I announced my plans, my manager made me this deal: He told me I had to use my own efforts to bring in fifteen confirmed bodies at two seminars a month, without using a newspaper ad.

If I was successful in doing that for six months, he would allow me to place an ad in the local newspaper at my own expense. Wow, what a huge disappointment that was for me. It meant I had to convince thirty people a month to show up at one of two events. And I had to confirm they showed up. Because I knew no one in town, it seemed like an insurmountable task.

I went to Hal and whined about my dilemma. He quickly told me the manager had made him the same "deal," and he basically told me to quit whining. Well, he didn't exactly say it that way because Hal was never untoward, but he gently encouraged me to get busy and get the job done. So I did. I made up flyers, had them compliance-approved, and started mailing them out to everyone and anyone on the small list I had compiled. Then

I went to the phone book and picked more names. That's really how scientific it was. I was very disciplined about calling each person on the mailing list exactly three days later, asking if they had received my flyer, and inquiring whether they were going to come to my seminar. It turned out that almost none of them had any recollection of receiving my flyer, so I struck up a conversation with them on the phone and just invited them to the seminar. If they didn't commit to the next seminar, I at least got them to be polite and consider coming to a future seminar. I knew I needed to get fifteen people to the next seminar, and I realized there would be a lot of no-shows, so I figured I needed to get twenty-five to thirty people to say yes the night before in order to get my fifteen. I would always call all the "yes" people the night before and remind them.

The night of the seminar, I would pray. Fortunately, I had many seminars with fifteen people, but not always. Sometimes there were four. Sometimes one. But I put on the same show no matter who attended. It was showtime and I needed to perform!

I gave my seminars, and lo and behold, a certain percentage of attendees agreed to meet with me. Then, a certain number of meetings ended up with the prospects becoming clients. I quickly learned it was a numbers game. The more people who attended, the more who set up meetings, and the more who became clients. It was as simple as that!

Whenever possible, I tried to get the follow-up appointment scheduled for the night of the seminar. Then the next day I called all the no-shows and reminded them about the seminar they had missed the night before. They usually displayed some kind of remorse for not showing up, and I would let them know when the next seminar would be and ask them to attend. More often than not, they did. Then I would call all the people who attended, and this was my script: "Hi, this is Erin Botsford, and I'm just calling to say thank you for coming to last night's seminar." And then I shut up. I learned that the next person who spoke "lost." If they spoke next, I seemed to get the appointment. If I got nervous and spoke to break the silence, I got nothing. That was a valuable lesson for me.

The interesting thing about this six-month exercise that was essentially forced upon me by my manager is that I probably learned more in those six months than in any six-month period of my career. As it turns out, my manager was exceptionally smart. He wasn't the ogre I made him out to be. He knew I needed to learn a valuable lesson: how to fill a room on my own, with no ad in the paper. True to his word, after six months, he allowed me to start running an ad in the local newspaper (at my own expense), but I also continued to invite people just as I had before. I had learned how to fill a room. The interesting part about the ad is that it was expensive and was very unpredictable in terms of results. Sometimes I would get a lot of people from the ad, but most times not. That being said, it seemed more qualified people came as a result of the ad but considering the fact that my phone prospecting list had been created from the white pages of the telephone book, it's not hard to figure out why the ad people were a little more qualified.

Valuable Lessons I Learned from Giving Seminars

- Don't rely on newspaper or radio ads. Figure out a way to fill a room with other methods. That might be a direct mail campaign or using a telemarketer.

- Giving a seminar is an art. You must first "disturb" the prospects about what they are currently doing. If you don't "disturb" them, there is no incentive for them to change.

- There needs to be a call to action at the end. Most advisors don't do this or if they do, they don't do it well.

- You need to have an assistant or someone there to book appointments for you. You will be glad-handing while the others leave.

- You MUST contact every person who attended within twenty-four hours of the seminar. First, call the no-shows early in the morning, and then call the others. Don't leave the office until everyone who attended has been called and asked for an appointment.

- The margin of returns drops off dramatically after forty-eight hours. If you have not scheduled an appointment before then, it's not going to happen.

- The seminar is just the beginning. Advisors often forget the purpose of the seminar and think holding the seminar is the goal. They often present the seminar and are so exhausted by all the work it took to get people to the event that they forget the seminar is just the first step. If they don't do the immediate follow-up, it was all for naught. As a guide:

- Put forty percent of your effort into filling the room.

- Put ten percent of your effort on the actual presentation.

- Put fifty percent of your effort on the follow-up.

- Truthfully, you need to give each of these steps one hundred percent of your effort, but this gives you an idea on the importance of follow-up.

- Give thought to the length of the seminar. I have seen advisors buy into seminar programs and offer to teach seminars or classes to the same people on multiple nights or in semester-long continuing education courses. My personal experience tells me a one-time seminar that lasts less than two hours is plenty. I have always said a seminar is purely a "tap dance" for credibility. Generally, the people who attend will decide in the first five to ten minutes whether they are going to do business with you.

- Go where the money is. Since I lived in a town where the average per capita income was $9,000 per year, I decided to find out where the money was and go there. It turned out the only money in town was in the hands of "snowbirds" who came to winter in Panama City. So, I gave daytime seminars at the public library, and I prayed each time for rain! (If it rained, the husbands would not play golf; instead, they would come to my seminars!)

I learned a lot in my first few years, and I credit my early success to the combination of all these prospecting methods. Each activity fed or helped foster the other. At one point early in my career, I was stopping at six businesses each week, setting up at least three lunches per week, and doing an average of six seminars a month with no assistance. Occasionally, I would get a friend to come with me to help at a seminar, or sometimes I would pay one of the women who worked in the office to be my assistant at night. I didn't have an assistant assigned to me until I had been in the business for almost four years!

HIGH ACTIVITY COUNTS

At some point in my first couple of years, my friend Mack Bland gave me some good advice. Mack was in the real estate business, and he saw how hard I was working. He saw the early mornings at the Chamber of Commerce meetings. He saw the lunch meetings and the seminars going late into the evening; he saw it all. He encouraged me by saying, "Erin, just keep up your activity level and the business will come." I guess it's sort of like the saying, "Sling enough mud and some of it will stick." In the end, it truly was the massive amount of activity I created that resulted in my being "rookie of the year" for my broker training class. While the average broker opened an average of seven new accounts per month, I averaged twenty-two new accounts each month for the first two years of my career. It didn't come easy, but it came—one account at a time. I say all of the above to encourage you. If I did it, then so can you!

MY CAREER EXPERIENCES ITS FIRST HICCUP—STARTING OVER!

As mentioned earlier, I started my career with a brokerage firm in Panama City, Florida. In my first calendar year, I remember making a whopping total of $14,997. I can tell you I have never worked so hard in my life. The next year I made a little over $40,000, which I considered terrific. By my third year, I had reached that magic $100,000 level. From my perspective, I felt like I had hit the "mother lode." I was making more than I had ever imagined! I finally had CPAs and other centers of influence referring business to me. I was working hard and experiencing what I considered great results.

About that time, my husband got out of the military and started working for American Airlines, based out of Dallas. It was time to move . . . again. I can't say I was the happiest spouse making yet another move, but keeping my marriage and family intact was important to me, so I bit the bullet and made the move to Plano, Texas, a suburb of Dallas. I stayed with the same brokerage firm but basically started all over again.

So guess what I did? I went to the Chamber of Commerce and introduced myself to the woman behind the counter and asked her out to lunch. I started the "Out-to-Lunch Bunch" all over again. I started giving seminars in Plano, beginning with public libraries and then larger venues like hotels. It was a little easier because I knew what to expect. Then again, it was really difficult because I knew what to expect. I was hauling flip charts and materials in and out of my car at all hours of the day and night, sometimes falling into bed late at night, only to start the routine all over again in the morning.

SPEAKING TO CLUBS AND ORGANIZATIONS

In addition to doing seminars, I made myself available as a speaker to local clubs and organizations. I went to the Chamber of Commerce and got a list of all the clubs and organizations within a twenty-five-mile radius from my office. I made up flyers, had them compliance-approved, and sent them out to the program chair of each organization. I learned a couple of things in doing this:

1. The program chair and all other organizational positions change at some point during the year, usually in May. They rarely update this information until about August. To be sure you catch someone who oversees booking speakers for that organization, you should send the same flyer out about every other month, because chances are, it will either be ignored or forwarded to the appropriate person.

2. At the beginning of the program chair's term, they are scrambling to find speakers; so, the closer you can time your solicitation to their new position, the better.

3. On the flyer, be sure to highlight that you are "available on short notice." Very frequently the program chair will be faced with the unpleasant reality of a speaker canceling at the last minute. Many have told me they hung on to my flyer because they wanted a backup plan if one of their speakers cancels. It actually worked in my favor a couple of times.

4. Know your audience. Know what the group is all about. I can tell you from personal experience how embarrassing it can be to speak on a topic that is controversial to the tenets of that particular club. To illustrate this point, I was invited last minute to a club called the Exchange Club. I had NO idea what they stood for. About five minutes before I was to speak, I asked my host what the Exchange Club was all about, and he told me they believed in "buying American." You have no idea how far my jaw dropped because my topic and all my props were about "global investing." In about five minutes, I figured out a way to turn my topic into something palatable to this group, but I could have alleviated my terror by doing a little bit of homework beforehand. This was in an era long before Google searches and Internet access, so I will cut myself some slack!

5. Have multiple topics you can speak about. Given to me by my initial manager, this was a huge lesson that worked throughout my career. Most organizations want you to talk for twenty or thirty minutes. I used ten, three-by-five cards and came up with a variety of topics that I could talk on for about ten minutes. Then, depending upon the makeup

of the group and the time allotted to me, I could pick and choose topics that might be appropriate for my audience.

VALUABLE PROSPECTING/MARKETING LESSONS

- Your clients will come from the pool you swim in.

As a rookie broker, I felt very uncomfortable prospecting for wealthy clients. I tended to prospect on the east side of Panama City, which was home to predominantly military people. I felt more comfortable in this circle because I was one of them. On the other hand, most of them, like me, had limited resources and certainly not mega dollars to invest with me. Somehow, I had this delusion that even though I was prospecting to military people on the east side of town, by some magic trick the people who would show up at my seminars and/or become clients would be wealthy people from the west side of town.

One of the more successful brokers, Augie Yankee, took me aside and taught me a great lesson. Without being rude or condescending, he said these words, "Erin, something I have noticed in the course of my career is that when I prospect on the east side of town, my clients generally come from the east side of town, but when I spend my time prospecting on the west side of town, that's where the bulk of my clients come from." He was pointing out the obvious: All the rich people lived on the west side of town, yet he noticed I was spending the bulk of my time prospecting on the east side of town. I had to admit he was right. I was prospecting poor people and wondered why I had no rich people . . . go figure!

- If you're not on the phone or you're not in front of a prospect or client—you're not making money.

Another lesson I learned early on came from one of my instructors from broker training, Marlyn Van Meter. She said, "If you're not on the phone or in front of someone, you are not making money."

Over the years, I saw so many advisors deluding themselves by doing activities that would not result in revenue. The most notorious activity I saw was advisors spending hours upon hours reading *The Wall Street Journal* from cover to cover or working on their Quotrons (that's what we had prior to computers).

Their excuse was that they wanted to be ready to answer questions from people who called them. The sad truth was that if they continued in this behavior and didn't do some form of prospecting, there wouldn't be anyone calling them, so the information they were picking up was irrelevant. We all need to know what is going on in the financial markets, but I suggest you do your reading before or after normal business hours.

- All methods of prospecting work if you stick with it.

The key is to constantly refine and fine-tune your strategies, based on your results. One of the biggest mistakes I have witnessed is not the prospecting system used, but the lack of dogged consistency and commitment to using and working the system.

- Immediate follow-up to a meeting or encounter of any kind is paramount.

For instance, if you meet someone at lunch at a restaurant, try to follow up with that person by sending an e-mail from your car while you sit in the parking lot. If they have come to your office, it is impressive if you follow up immediately, so they have an e-mail from you by the time they return to their office.

- There is nothing that will ever replace the power of a handwritten note.

Even if you have followed up by sending an e-mail, if you really want to get their attention, follow that up with a handwritten note, addressed by you and stamped with a real stamp. That form of communication is becoming priceless.

For more information and additional resources, go to www.erinbotsford.com.

QUESTIONS TO PONDER:

- **What kind of prospecting appeals to you?**

If you knew you would have guaranteed success using any of the prospecting methods I mentioned, which type of prospecting method would you gravitate toward?

- **Are you consistent in your prospecting efforts?**

You cannot be willy nilly in your prospecting activities. You must be consistent and disciplined, realizing any marketing or prospecting activity you do today may not pay off for eighteen months to two years. As much as anything, the spoils go to the one who can hang in there long enough to see their efforts rewarded. While each prospecting or marketing activity needs to be evaluated and tweaked, don't just "try" something and quit after three or four months. I don't know of any activity that pays off in that short a time. I had people who came to me who had seen me speak seven, ten, even twenty years prior! Make an impression, and when the timing is right for the prospect, they will seek you out.

- **Do you need to become a better public speaker?**

Public speaking is considered a very scary thing; many people fear it. I have seen financial advisors invite wholesalers to do their public speaking for them.

The advisor just fills the room with prospects. Have you ever considered when the speaker walks off the stage, he takes his credibility with him? If you hate public speaking and think that solves your problem, think again. I would consider getting training or coaching to overcome the fear of public speaking, instead, especially if seminars are part of your marketing strategy. Keep the credibility; don't let it walk out the door. That being said, once the prospect becomes a client, there is nothing wrong with having outside speakers present various topics. Just make sure that you are the one introducing them, welcoming your clients, and closing out the event.

CHAPTER 5

CREATING YOUR BRAND

If you want your financial services business to grow, flourish, and withstand the test of time, you MUST find ways to stand out from the crowd. Differentiate yourself from your competitors by creating a unique tool or unique value proposition—or both—to deliver to your clients. If you are not sure how to do this, I will provide examples in this chapter and explain the psychology behind each.

Don't consider this a one-time exercise, however. Make sure that whatever you use to differentiate your business today continues to evolve over time. Everything connected to your brand must be updated regularly so it stays relevant. Be sure to freshen *everything*—from your logos to your website to your pocket folders to the pens you give your clients at meetings—at least every three years. (Consider how frequently design trends change; you don't want your materials to look outdated.) The good news is that few advisors do this part well, so if you spend some time on this, you can significantly stand out from the crowd.

DIFFERENTIATION IS ESSENTIAL

From day one, I realized I needed a way to set myself apart from all my competitors. In fact, I had extra incentive to come up with creative ways to impress my prospects and clients because I wasn't going to give my first boss the satisfaction of seeing me fail.

Fortunately, I made a very important discovery while working through my first set of cold calls. As I listened to the individuals on the other end of the line, it occurred to me that most prospects already had at least one relationship with someone else in the industry. The question was (and it is the same today), "How could I distinguish myself, so prospects know that I have something unique and noteworthy to offer?" How could I pique their interest?

I started noticing that my competitors always used pie chart asset allocations, as if it were a tool required by the regulators. Since I had started as a stockbroker, investments and asset allocations were about the only thing we addressed on a daily basis. My first question to myself was, "How can I jazz up this boring pie chart?" My second question to myself was, "Could I accurately show a person's recommended asset allocation without using a pie chart?"

About the same time, I heard a saying, "In the absence of differentiation, you become irrelevant." Those words always seemed to float across my mind, so I decided to create something different from the traditional pie chart asset allocation models.

That's how I came up with what I called the **GRID**™ form of asset allocation. The timing on this was probably a little bit before Morningstar's nine-box grid became popular. In fact, I'm sure I had never seen Morningstar's grid when I created my **GRID**™, or I would have probably used theirs! It's important to also note the context of that time. When I started in the business (in the late '80s), there was no such thing as the Internet. Morningstar rankings came in very large black notebooks with thin papers for each mutual fund ranking. These sheets were updated every quarter. Since subscriptions to Morningstar were relatively expensive, not all firms bought the subscription, and even those that did, didn't necessarily supply that information to all their local offices.

Back then, *we* were the keepers and protectors of all information concerning stocks, bonds, and mutual funds; that was the fun part of the business. Until the Internet came around, we had way more access to information than our clients did. Once the Internet came into existence, it seemed our clients sometimes had access to more information than we did!

The first GRID™ I created only had four boxes (see Image 3.1).

I initially named the boxes "Large Cap," "Mid Cap," "Small Cap" and "Bonds." Sometimes my Grid was labeled "Stocks," "Bonds," "Real Estate," and "Cash." The labels I used depended upon what I was trying to demonstrate to the client. What I noticed from a psychological standpoint was the more buckets there were on the piece of paper, the more inclined people were to write bigger checks. So, if you had one bucket, you would get X amount of dollars. If you had two buckets, you'd get twice as much. If you had four buckets, then you'd get four times as much! I have to assume the client reasoned that it was safer to diversify his or her assets into as many buckets as possible!

Original **GRID**™ Asset Allocation

Large Cap Stocks		Mid Cap Stocks	
Total Value	**$0**	**Total Value**	**$0**
% of Portfolio		% of Portfolio	
Small Cap Stocks		Bonds/Fixed Income	
Total Value	**$0**	**Total Value**	**$0**
% of Portfolio		% of Portfolio	

or

Stocks		Bonds	
Total Value	**$0**	**Total Value**	**$0**
% of Portfolio		% of Portfolio	
Real Estate		Cash	
Total Value	**$0**	**Total Value**	**$0**
% of Portfolio		% of Portfolio	

*Image 3.1: Original forms of the **GRID**™ asset allocation*

At first, I started with four buckets and experimented with which asset classes to include. Then I got a little more serious about creating a viable alternative to pie charts. In my study of the markets, I determined back then that there was a minimum of eight asset classes that should be considered in a balanced portfolio. Hence, my second version of the **GRID**™ contained two quadrants with four asset classes in each (Image 3.2).

Botsford Financial Group's **GRID**™ Asset Allocation

DOMESTIC POSITIONS: **INTERNATIONAL POSITIONS:**

Large Cap Stocks/ Growth & Income	Mid Cap/Growth	Large Cap Stocks/ Growth & Income	Mid Cap/Growth
Total Value $0 % of Portfolio	Total Value $0 % of Portfolio	Total Value $0 % of Portfolio	Total Value $0 % of Portfolio
Aggressive Growth/ Small Cap/Sector	**Cash/Bonds/Fixed Income**	**Aggressive Growth/ Small Cap/Sector**	**Emerging Markets**
Total Value $0 % of Portfolio	Total Value $0 % of Portfolio	Total Value $0 % of Portfolio	Total Value $0 % of Portfolio

Image 3.2: Second iteration of the **GRID**™ *asset allocation*

On the left-hand side, the grid allocated space for all their domestic positions, and on the right-hand side, it allocated space for all their international positions. Looking at Image 3.2, on the upper left, you will see the categories I used: "Large Cap;" "Mid Cap;" "Small Cap;" plus "Cash, Bonds, and Fixed Income." On the right-hand side, the grid allocated space for their international positions. The international categories I used were "Large Cap," "Mid Cap," "Small Cap," and "Emerging Markets."

My **GRID**™ form of asset allocation proved to be an invaluable asset. It showed, at a glance, how different my firm's approach was from our competitors' approach. We made sure to update it regularly, so the grid evolved many times over the years.

THE PROBLEM WITH PIE CHARTS

Let me explain why my **GRID**™ form of asset allocation was viewed as better than a pie chart. Have you ever seen a pie chart asset allocation that reminded you of Pac-Man (Image 3.3)?

Traditional Pie Chart Allocation

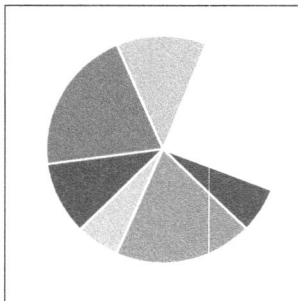

Image 3.3: Traditional pie charts fail to indicate what asset classes have been excluded—intentionally or unintentionally.

Of course not! A pie chart must add up to one hundred percent or it looks like an incomplete asset allocation. But a pie chart does not show clients what they **don't** have or what has been left out of the recommendation. It is, by its nature, an incomplete picture. And yet, I found that 99.9 percent of the time, my competitors came to the table armed with a pie chart.

With the **GRID**™, there are predetermined categories that should be considered in every portfolio. That doesn't mean every asset class will or should be selected, but it should be considered. Perhaps a particular client does not want any exposure to emerging markets. Then that quadrant would have a ZERO in it. That's fine. The point is we considered the asset class, and we chose not to include it. It very easily shows up as a missing category because it has a ZERO in the column. Pie charts have no zeros, so they have no way of demonstrating what is missing.

Here's a real example of how I used my **GRID**™ to win a client.

In the mid-1990s, I had a prospect—a Delta airline pilot who had recently retired. He had several million dollars to invest. He came to me and said, "Erin, I want to see, based on my goals and objectives, what you would do using $1 million, as an example. What I'm going to do is get a proposal from one other advisor whom I've been talking to, and I'm going to show you his proposal and show him your proposal." I thought it was interesting that he told me that, because the truth is most prospects do visit with multiple advisors, probably more so than they did twenty-five years ago.

It was the first time in my career someone was actually honest about that with me, so I said, "Fair enough," and agreed to the challenge. I told him I would like to see my competitor's proposal first. He said, "That's fine." I could have bet and won a lot of money, simply by predicting the kind of asset allocation model my competitor would propose. Of course, it was a pie chart (see Image 3.4)! All I did was take my competitor's pie chart and plot what he was proposing on my grid.

His proposal recommended allocating that $1 million in the following way:

Competitor's Retirement Portfolio
Proposal $1,000,000

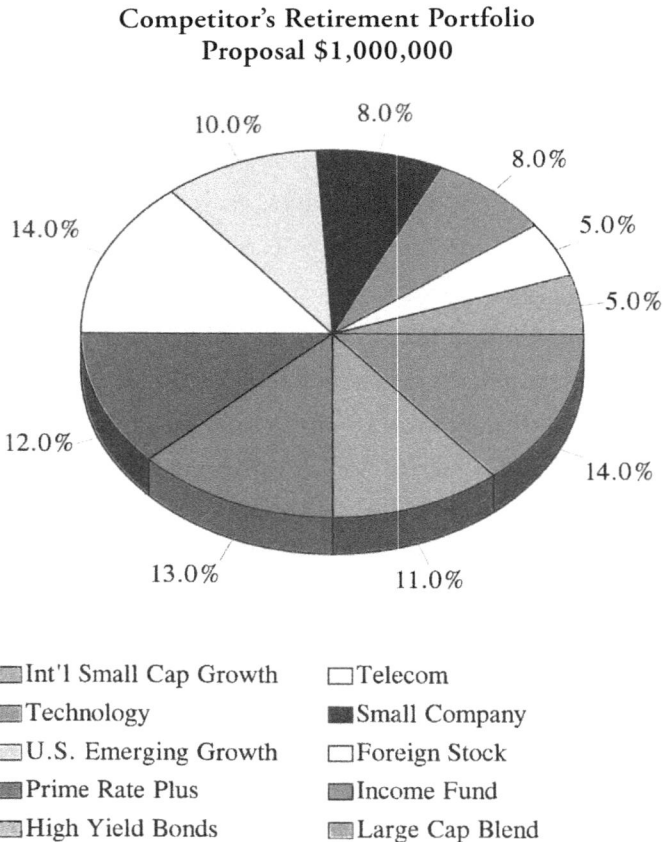

Legend:

- Int'l Small Cap Growth
- Technology
- U.S. Emerging Growth
- Prime Rate Plus
- High Yield Bonds
- Telecom
- Small Company
- Foreign Stock
- Income Fund
- Large Cap Blend

Image 3.4: Competitor's investment proposal as it came in a pie chart asset allocation

THE COMPETITOR'S PROPOSAL
VS THE WINNING PROPOSAL

This case ended up being very easy to win. All I did was convert the numbers/percentages that showed up on my competitor's pie chart to my **GRID**™ form of asset allocation (see Image 3.5). I won that client because I was able to clearly demonstrate that my competitor had completely discounted or left out a number of asset classes.

Competitor's Proposal on "The **GRID**™"
Proposed Asset Allocation: $1,000,000

DOMESTIC POSITIONS: $680,000   68.0%   **INTERNATIONAL POSITIONS: $320,000   32.0%**

Large Cap Stocks/ Growth & Income	Mid Cap/Growth		Large Cap Stocks/ Growth & Income	Mid Cap/Growth	
0	Mid Cap Value	$140,000	Int'l Growth $140,000	0	
Total Value $ -	**Total Value $140, 000**		**Total Value $140, 000**	**Total Value $ -**	
% of Portfolio 0.0%	**% of Portfolio 14.0%**		**% of Portfolio 14.0%**	**% of Portfolio 0.0%**	
Aggressive Growth/ Small Cap/Sector	Cash/Bonds/ Fixed Income		Aggressive Growth/ Small Cap/Sector	Emerging Markets	
Emerging Growth $100,000	Prime Plus $120,000		Global Tech $80,000	0	
Small Growth $80,000	Income Fund $130,000		Global Telecom $50,000		
	High Income Bond $110,000		Global Small Co $50,000		
Total Value $180,000	**Total Value $360,000**		**Total Value $180,000**	**Total Value $ -**	
% of Portfolio 18.0%	**% of Portfolio 36.0%**		**% of Portfolio 18.0%**	**% of Portfolio 0.0%**	

*Image 3.5: Competitor's Proposal on Our **GRID**™*

More importantly, because my competitor had used a pie chart, the prospect had no way to know which asset classes had been left out. You will then see what I proposed (see Image 3.6). Since I could always count on the competition to use a pie chart, my **GRID**™ form of asset allocation made it relatively easy to differentiate myself from the competition. It proved to be one of the best differentiation tools I created.

Botsford Financial Group's Proposal
Proposed Asset Allocation: $1,000,000

DOMESTIC POSITIONS: $800,000 80.0%			
Large Cap Stocks/ Growth & Income		**Mid Cap/Growth**	
Large Growth	$200,000	Mid Cap Growth	$100,000
Large Value	$100,000	Mid Cap Value	$100,000
Total Value	$300,000	Total Value	$200,000
% of Portfolio	30.0%	% of Portfolio	20.0%
Aggressive Growth/ Small Cap/Sector		**Cash/Bonds/ Fixed Income**	
Small Growth	$40,000	Prime Plus	$100,000
Samll Value	$40,000	Income Fund	$50,000
Sector	$20,000	High Income Bond	$50,000
Total Value	$100,000	Total Value	$200,000
% of Portfolio	10.0%	% of Portfolio	20.0%

INTERNATIONAL POSITIONS: $200,000 20.0%			
Large Cap Stocks/ Growth & Income		**Mid Cap/Growth**	
Int'l Large Growth	$50,000	Int'l Mid Growth	$25,000
Int'l Large Value	$50,000	Int'l Mid Value	$25,000
Total Value	$100,000	Total Value	$50,000
% of Portfolio	10.0%	% of Portfolio	5.0%
Aggressive Growth/ Small Cap/Sector		**Emerging Markets**	
Int'l Smallcap	$25,000	Emerging Markets	$25,000
Total Value	$25,000	Total Value	$25,000
% of Portfolio	2.5%	% of Portfolio	2.5%

Image 3.6: Botsford Financial Group's Winning Proposal on the **GRID**™

BLOCKS PLAN—A GREAT WAY TO OVERCOME HIDDEN EMOTIONAL BARRIERS TO MOVING FORWARD!

Another unique tool we created is something we called our "Blocks Plan." Back in 1995–1996, I started working with the senior executives of a major Fortune 500 company. In 1999, the company went public and ended up tripling the value of its company stock. The employee who thought he would retire with $3 million in stock now had $9 million. The guy who thought he would have $5 million now had $15 million.

While working with more than two hundred of these executives, we discovered most of them had never done much in the way of comprehensive financial planning. In fact, many of them had ninety percent of their net worth in this single publicly traded stock. Their other largest asset was typically their personal residence.

As you might imagine, these executives were extremely loyal to their employer and their stock. You could even go so far as to say they felt an emotional attachment to the stock. Therefore, they were exceptionally reluctant to sell large portions of their stock all at once, even though they knew it was the smartest move financially. Emotion had clouded their thinking. It didn't seem to matter that this was during the dot-com era and companies like Enron, MCI WorldCom, and Sprint had their stock prices fall dramatically, some even to zero. It didn't seem to matter that dozens of companies had gone completely out of existence. They weren't looking at this through the lens of logic. From an emotional standpoint, they just weren't ready to part with company stock.

This was understandable. Some had worked for the company for thirty-five years. The company had not only paid them twice a month for those thirty-five years, it had also given them stock, and now the stock had made them rich.

The IPO for this company was very popular, so there was a lot of competition in the marketplace for these clients from other advisors. We started seeing proposals from our competitors recommending that clients sell fifty to seventy-five percent of their company stock immediately after the IPO and reposition the proceeds into managed money or mutual funds. No one could argue with the viability of those proposals, but there was no way these clients were going to do that. Their loyalty to the company was just too strong.

I was concerned because I held myself out as a certified financial planner. With that designation came a fiduciary responsibility to do the right thing and give the right advice. Everyone knows holding ninety percent of your net worth in a single publicly traded stock is not the right thing to do. At first, however, we were no more persuasive than our competitors in convincing these executives to sell large portions of their stock.

One morning, I went for a long run, and the solution came to me. I created the "Blocks Plan." It was a very strategic way to get around the resistance we had repeatedly encountered when we recommended that executives sell $5 million of their stock right now. Rather than fight that losing battle, we created a plan that would sell tranches (portions) of stock at predefined price points.

We called the tranches "blocks."

We would say, "Mr. Client, your stock is trading at $70 a share.

Chapter 5: Creating Your Brand   97

To meet your retirement income needs, we have calculated you will need to reposition $5 million of your stock. You can sell all $5 million now or we can sell in blocks, such as $1 million worth of stock at $70 a share, $1 million worth when it hits $72.50, $1 million worth at $75, $1 million worth at $77.50, and $1 million worth at $80 per share. Can you agree that, if and when it hits these price points, it would make sense to sell these amounts?" That was a much more palatable suggestion or recommendation than to sell $5 million today.

Usually, we separated the stock positions into five blocks. Sometimes, if the price went up quickly, we might sell three blocks at one time because those target prices had been reached.

In addition, we had a plan to sell a certain amount if the stock started declining in value. They essentially agreed to a drop-dead price point. If it fell to that point, they agreed to sell all $5 million. They were convinced the stock price would never fall, so getting them to agree to a drop-dead price was really not an issue. That being said, we certainly didn't want to risk another Sprint or WorldCom situation, where some of their employees rode the stocks all the way down to the bottom.

The Blocks Plan actually worked out very well. In fact, we soon realized we had coined a term. Not only did our clients use this term, but we found out our competitors referred to their shares as blocks as well. The word itself helped those executives gain a measure of detachment. We were no longer referring to the stock as "stock," but "blocks," which seemed much more palatable to the client. It proved to be very successful at helping clients do something they knew they needed to do but weren't comfortable doing.

YOUR RULES—YOUR BRAND

I was in this business for over three decades. One thing that kept it fun and "fresh" for me was changing things up when there was a good reason to do so. A business has to evolve if it is to thrive over the long term. One time a coach of mine said, "You get to set the rules for the people you are going to work with, and you're allowed to change those rules."

In the decades I was in business, I changed the rules of my practice many, many times. I would draw a proverbial line in the sand and say, "From now on, these are the new rules of my business, and this is how I'm going to work going forward." I laid out the rules to the next potential client, and if they accepted the terms of my business proposition, they were allowed to become a client. If they didn't agree to those terms, they were not a good fit for our business.

When I first started in the business, I wasn't really aware that I needed to have rules or set boundaries for my business—what I would or would not do, how much I would charge, whom I would accept as a client, etc. Early in my career, I basically took anyone who could fog a mirror as a client and jumped through hoops for them day or night. As time went on, I realized this was no way to run a business. However, back then there were very few people who trained, mentored, or coached people like me on business or practice management.

Yes, there were seminars offered by wholesalers, and these wholesalers said we needed to create account minimums. So I created account minimums. There was definitely a movement encouraging a shift from commission-based business to charging a percentage of assets under management. Even under that model, however, most of us did a lot of work for free. We did research, typed up proposals, and presented our ideas only to see our ideas go down the street to Schwab.

With the advance of the Internet and a raging bull market in the late 1990s, many individual investors were convinced they could invest all on their own. We started seeing clients come in for free advice and taking their business elsewhere. Even the results from my seminars started to wane. The people attending seminars in the mid- to late-1990s became "tire-kickers." They came to eat the free cookies and get free advice, but my closing ratio following those seminars really went down. It was quite depressing. What was more depressing was that I was doing a lot of work, meeting with prospects, typing up proposals, and sharing my ideas, but to no avail.

I began to feel resentful that the financial services industry allowed this culture to emerge over time. No one expected their attorney or CPA to work for free. I consoled myself by thinking about my realtor friends who also spent a lot of money on gas and a lot of time showing people property, with no guarantee that they would get the sale.

Finally, in 1997, I received mentoring from a woman named Amy Leavitt, and things changed dramatically for me. Under her tutelage, I learned the value of charging a financial planning fee and an annual renewal fee, which is how my business would be positioned thereafter. I am not talking about charging an "assets under management" fee. This is a fee for creating an investment plan or a comprehensive financial plan.

Before 1997, no client had ever paid me a fee to create a financial plan. I decided to draw a line in the sand and said, "I'm not going to change the rules on the existing people who work with me because that's not fair, but I am going to set up a new set of rules for everybody that comes in from this day forward." So, from January 1997 going forward, I said I would only take clients who would pay me a financial planning fee.

What I've found is that when you tell your clients what your rules are up front, either they accept them or they don't. For instance, in one of my many rule changes, we decided to charge a financial planning fee and mandated that the entire fee be paid up front. I also told clients that each year we would charge a renewal fee going forward. The interesting thing is that the clients are always okay with your rules. Planners are the ones who generally have an issue with creating and articulating their own rules. So each year from that point forward, we sent an invoice, and they sent a check. There was no pushback because we set the stage and outlined the rules up front.

My first financial planning fee was only $250. By the end, my minimum financial planning fee ended up at $7,500, to be paid in advance. We frequently charged many multiples of that minimum fee based on the client and the complexity of the case. I only point that out so you can see the evolution of our practice. Every incremental increase in our planning fee was technically a change in the rules. I actually liked changing the rules. It meant I was making progress and was more in charge of my world and my outcome.

Remember, at one point, the clients got me and all my advice for free! Then I started charging them a $250 planning fee, but they still got me. Fast-forward about two decades, and by the end, they were charged $7,500 or more, and no one got me; they got the even more brilliant people on my team! So you see, there have been many changes along the way. The key is to never be afraid to draw a new line in the sand. It's healthy for you and for your business. Typically, I liked to change my rules on January 1 of each year. It tended to coincide with my New Year's resolutions.

LIFESTYLE DRIVEN INVESTING™

My signature piece of intellectual property—the one that allowed me to become a best-selling author—is the trademarked concept, "Lifestyle Driven Investing™." Clearly described in my book *The Big Retirement Risk: Running Out of Money Before You Run Out of Time*, Lifestyle Driven Investing™ is simple, yet profound.

It was proven to work in the most difficult of market melt-downs (the dot-com bubble and the 2008 financial collapse), which is why I decided to write a book about it. The premise is this: To fund a client's Preferred Lifestyle™, you should first segregate their retirement expenses into various categories. We call the categories "Needs," "Wants," "Likes," and "Wishes." Once their expenses are categorized, our process was as follows:

- Fund their **Needs** with what we call "Lifestyle" invest-ments. The category is merely a filter for evaluating any type of investment. In order to be considered a Lifestyle investment, it must produce an income, either now or in the future. That income MUST BE **safe** or **predictable** or **guaranteed**. If none of those descriptors fit, it is not a Lifestyle investment.

- Fund their **Wants** with what we call "hybrid" investments. Again, there is no such thing as a hybrid investment. The name is a filter through which we evaluate the attributes of an investment we are considering. To be considered a hybrid, the investment must produce an income. But, in this case, we could likely never say the income was safe or predictable or guaranteed.

- Fund their **Likes** and **Wishes** with "non-Lifestyle" investments. Non-Lifestyle investments are the broadest category. They would include all the traditional investment products, such as stocks, bonds, mutual funds, ETFs, hedge funds, private equity, and managed futures. Anything tied to a market that can move would be considered a non-Lifestyle investment. Other private investments, like real estate, oil wells, venture capital, etc., would all be non-Lifestyle investments. When our clients had all their needs and wants funded, we encouraged them to be as aggressive as they wanted to be with the rest of their money. Since none of it was earmarked for their ongoing lifestyle needs, they could use these dollars for capital appreciation opportunities they would likely never have considered if they had been doing traditional investing by using Modern Portfolio Theory or systematic withdrawals from a balanced portfolio. Again, the entire strategy is well documented in my book. I hope you will take the time to read it.

I will admit I was very honored when Dr. Wade Pfau, professor at The American College of Financial Services, referenced my concept of "Lifestyle Driven Investing™" as a second school of thought, falling under what he calls the "safety first" approach. Dr. Pfau has been teaching financial advisors across the country, so I am hopeful Lifestyle Driven Investing™ will catch on. It certainly served my client base well.

THE BIG RETIREMENT RISK: RUNNING OUT OF MONEY BEFORE YOU RUN OUT OF TIME

While I am on the subject of smart ways to set yourself apart from your competitors, let me tell you how powerful it can be to write your own book. I'll be honest—writing my first book was the most difficult and expensive exercise I have ever undertaken. However, it was also the most fulfilling project and the single best tool I could have created to help leverage our business. I credit the book with catapulting our business to a level I had always dreamed about.

Imagine walking in the front door of your office and seeing a total stranger sitting there, waiting to meet with one of your advisors. They did not come to a seminar; they did not request to meet with you. Or imagine you are on a local TV show as a guest and someone calls in wanting to work with your firm, based on having seen you on TV and then having bought your book. That's when you know you have truly arrived. That's what my first book did for my business.

Once people read the book and agreed with our firm's philosophy of money, they were much more likely to be willing to meet with one of my advisors. The book became the ultimate tool for leveraging my business. There are some very big pluses in being a published author:

- It gives you immediate credibility.

- It opens doors to other types of media opportunities, such as radio, TV, and magazine articles. In fact, I was asked (and I agreed) to be the celebrity guest on a ten-day Mediterranean cruise shortly after the book came out! We sent out one e-mail and ended up having forty-six clients and friends join us on the cruise.

- It creates amazing leverage. When people read my book and understood my philosophy about money, they would "get us" and have no issue meeting with one of my advisors rather than with me. In the years after the book was published, I met with very few of the actual prospects who eventually became clients.

- It more than pays for itself. As I said earlier, completing the book cost me a considerable amount of time and money. It was a big investment. That said, the book paid for itself in more than monetary ways and gave me more freedom than I had ever imagined.

We created many more proprietary tools over my three-decade career—some that are still used by my former firm and some that were shelved. The key is continuing to create and bring about innovations in your business. Most advisors are not very good at this, so it's really not hard to stand out from your competitors. Most advisors tend to use their home office marketing material and collateral pieces, which end up looking like everyone else's. It takes a little more effort to differentiate yourself from the rest of the pack, but I can tell you it pays off in spades.

For more information and additional resources, go to www. erinbotsford.com.

QUESTIONS TO PONDER:

- **What is YOUR unique method or unique value proposition?**

  You MUST find ways to stand out from the crowd. Differentiate yourself from your competitors by creating a unique tool or unique value proposition—or both—to deliver to your clients.

- **Do you have a different way of demonstrating things to your clients or prospects?**

  Is there a way you could distinguish yourself, so prospects know that you have something unique and noteworthy to offer? How could you pique their interest?

- **What sets you apart from your competitors?**

  Consider your products, terminology, salesmanship, or presentation style. Are there areas where you're unique? Is there a chance for you to take something tried and true and make it new and singular for your clients?

- **People value what they pay for: Are you working for free?**

  Is it time to review your brand, rules, processes, and pricing structures? If you don't value your talents and skills, then nobody else will either.

CHAPTER 6

BUILDING A TEAM

I have heard it said that there are two ways to create a business. One, you can be a technician, like Bill Gates, where you create a product and then hire salespeople to go out and sell that product. Or, second, you can be an entrepreneur like me and surround yourself with technicians who work on the cases as they come in. In my case, those technicians normally did a far better job than me on the technical side of the business.

Clearly, either way to grow a business will work. However, as one of my mentors, Michael Gerber, points out in his book *The E-Myth Revisited,* financial advisor must be three things when *launching* a business:

1. They must be the hunter/rainmaker/salesperson—the one who goes out and brings in the business.
2. They also have to be the manager. They must manage the financial planning process initially and eventually manage the people who work for them.
3. They must be the technician; they have to do the actual work of the business, which is creating the financial plan.

In the beginning, when you first start in this business, you have to do all those things. Most of us tend to do all those things until we reach our first "ceiling of complexity," a term coined by Dan Sullivan. This ceiling occurs when there are no more hours in the day, and you can do no more to grow the business by yourself. This is the first great inflection point, where you realize that, in order to grow, you must hire other people to work for you.

If you excel at being the hunter/rainmaker/salesperson, then that's great; only a small percentage of people in the world actually have the hunter DNA. This skill is essential to building a business. If you can't continually bring in new clients, you won't be in business for very long. Regardless of how satisfied you may be with the business you have now and your current income, natural attrition and commoditization of our industry make it necessary to continually bring in new clients. As they say: "If a business is not growing, it is dying . . ."

Realize, however, that replicating your function as a hunter will be the most challenging part of growing your business. When you finally find someone who has that strength, it often and quickly becomes painfully clear that the new hunter's intent is to learn from you and then go build something for him or herself. Because this is true, it is wise to have a rock-solid non-compete/non-solicitation agreement in place. Your first step should be to hire people to do the technical work of the business (to create the financial plans and to service the clients you bring in). This gives you the bandwidth to bring in more and more clients for your team to advise and service. Once the team is in place and you have a stable of happy clients, you can put systems and processes in place so that your internal team can foster warm referrals from the existing clients they are helping.

The bottom line is this: If you want to grow your business, then you have to build a team. Hiring the first person is the most difficult of all the hiring decisions. It's also the one you should consider the most carefully. Your goal is to train one person and then have them train the second, third, and fourth employees. There are a couple of reasons why you want to build a team, but in the end, it's all about leveraging. It's very difficult to "build the business of your dreams" with just you. Again, if it's all about you, then all you really have is a job; you don't have a business. If the business is totally reliant upon you showing up each day, then you don't have a business that has any intrinsic value. You just have a friendly boss . . . you.

To go into these concepts in much greater depth, I highly recommend that you read Gerber's *The E-Myth Revisited*. I agree with almost everything in that book. Several years ago, I was privileged to follow Michael Gerber as a speaker at an industry conference to outline the ways in which I incorporated his principles in my financial services business.

WORK ON YOUR BUSINESS, NOT IN YOUR BUSINESS

This is one of Michael's major themes: Building a team allows you to *work* ON *your business instead of* IN *your business*. This point is so important that I frequently reference these two quotes from Michael's book:

> "If you want to work in a business go to work
> for someone else, because while you're doing all
> the work, you're not working on your busi-
> ness. You're not doing the strategic work of the
> business."[2]

and

> "Most people who own businesses in this
> country work far more than they should for the
> return they're getting. The problem is, they're
> doing the wrong work."[3]

The one thing I find interesting about the financial services industry is that you don't see many financial advisors who have what I would refer to as a bona fide business. Michael Gerber is the one who opened my eyes to this. So let me repeat: A business is not really a business if it relies upon you. If you have to be there every day, if you're the one meeting with all the clients, then you don't really own a business; you've simply bought yourself a job. If I were you, I would ask myself, "Do I really own a business, or have I just bought myself a job?" Try not to fool yourself with that answer. There's nothing inherently wrong with either answer to the question, but it's very difficult to grow a large practice and

---

2. Michael E. Gerber, *The E-Myth Revisited: Why Most Small Businesses Don't Work and What to Do About It* (New York: HarperCollins, 2001).

3. Gerber, *The E-Myth, Revisited.*

have the life of your dreams if your life is always consumed by doing the day-to-day work of the business.

LEVERAGE: THE MOST IMPORTANT CONCEPT

In his book, Michael Gerber wisely advocates comparing your business to McDonald's. He talks about the founder, Ray Kroc, and the creation of the fast-food franchise model. Ray's company was in the business of serving fast food to large numbers of individuals. He started in one store and likely worked in that store, initially as the "hunter" (the one who brings in customers), the manager, and the technician. Ray Kroc eventually grew the business exponentially by creating systems and processes to do the "work" of the business and hiring people to run those systems and processes.

How does this apply to you? Well, if you want to build a business that can operate without your day-to-day involvement, you have to first build a team and then create systems and processes that allow your team to service your clients and run the day-to-day operations of your business. That creates "leverage," the most important concept to master if you want to build a large, successful practice.

To that end, I'd like to share some truisms coach Dan Sullivan shared that were eye-openers. I hope they'll be the same for you:

"If you want to make $300 an hour, stop doing $20 an hour work."

> "You can do anything in the world as long as you're not the one doing it."

In our business, the clients need to be served. The question is: Do they need to be served by you? I am living proof. I had a large practice with two offices, and there wasn't one client who expected to work directly with me. In fact, through all the financial crises and calamities, I received very few calls from clients. Normally, the only time I heard from a client was to give me a referral. That's the way it should be for you too. Don't worry; you can get there, and there are people like me who want to help you get there quickly!

A DIFFERENT WORLD FOR ME TODAY

Thanks to people like Paul, Dan Sullivan, and Michael Gerber, I ended up playing fewer roles in the firm. Like Paul, my main function was to be a rainmaker. I continued to try to create new and different ways to expose our firm to people who didn't know about us. As we grew, we hired new "hunters" whom I trained and mentored. As I said earlier, finding hunters who want to work within my firm was a challenge, but it can be done. We had to find people who wanted to build a "firm," not their own practice. Also, I continued to work with my management team to provide vision, leadership, and creativity. Annually, I worked with the entire team to set goals for the business, including annual revenue and profitability goals. I was still the de facto leader of the firm but to the largest extent possible, I let my management team run the day-to-day operations. Clearly, when difficult decisions had to be made, the buck stopped at my door, but I always asked my management team to weigh in on what they would do. My goal was always to "work myself out of a job."

Other than those limited activities, the business ran well without me, which is a testament to the great people I managed to hire over the years. It didn't start out that way. It was an evolutionary process. However, with patience and persistence, you, too, can build a business that can run day-to-day operations without requiring your direct involvement. After all, isn't a business supposed to be the benefactor that allows you to live a great life? For most people, their business IS their life. I know; that's where I started.

TEAM BUILDING

To create the business of your dreams, you must hire qualified people to work for you. Most on our team were Series 7, Series 65, and insurance licensed so they were legally allowed to discuss financial products with clients. Every employee, except for our receptionist and our bookkeeper, had to have the appropriate securities and insurance licenses to be part of my team.

In the beginning, there are a few things you will likely want to continue to do, at least while you build the infrastructure of your business.

1. **Bring in clients**. It is likely you will always be a primary rainmaker for your firm. Your job will be to find and sell your company's value proposition to good-quality prospects.

Be sure to clearly define your market and not waste time on people who don't fit the profile of your ideal client.

2. **Socialize with clients**. If you do things correctly, you will have positioned your business so clients enjoy working with qualified members of your team. Eventually, your licensed staff should be able to do nearly everything, including conducting quarterly reviews and making product recommendations. Although I eventually let go of those tasks, I continued to socialize with our clients, something I very much enjoyed doing. In fact, it kept me connected to my purpose, which is taking care of people.

As I said before, it takes time to upgrade your business so that it works without your day-to-day involvement. It also takes a different mindset: You have to be willing to let go of more and more and slowly relinquish the role of always being the "go-to" person. (In the next chapter, I'll talk about how to make this transition more comfortable for your existing clients.)

When I first made this transition, I stayed very involved in the process in the first year. While I did not sit in on all client meetings, I generally did attend any meetings where new opportunities were likely to be discussed. Yes, I was reluctant to turn over the relationship to my licensed staff, but I had another purpose too. I felt like I needed to be in those meetings to critique the communication skills of my staff, which worked out well. After every meeting, we would discuss what went on in the meeting. I would point out obvious missteps and make suggestions for the next meeting. It took some time.

Also, one thing I have always enjoyed doing, and still do today, is taking new clients out to dinner. Once they had implemented our plan, my husband and I would take them to dinner. We enjoyed breaking bread with our clients, and we felt it strengthened the relationship with our firm. It also gave me the chance to solicit feedback on our team and our process so we could continually improve.

As the "creative genius" of the business, I still participated in the strategic planning of the business. I was always looking for the next "big thing" for the business. The next big thing may have been a new financial product that had been created in the marketplace; other times, it might have been doing joint venture marketing with other professionals. I also loved spending time training and motivating my team. It's so gratifying to see my team members grow in their knowledge and skill.

MY TEAM MEMBERS WERE MY PARTNERS

When it came to our team, I tried to treat all team members as if they were my business partners, because, in essence, they were. Here is my advice to create that environment:

1. Always back your team even if it means letting go of a client. Your team is more important than any single client.

2. Let your team members do their job. Don't micromanage them. Your team will rise to the level of your expectations and, with a little encouragement, will greatly exceed your expectations.

3. Give up some control. I think the main reason people don't progress is because they cannot give up control.

4. Create a way for your team members to participate in the profitability of the business. My team members were rewarded based on the success of the firm. All team members had a base salary, but after one year with the firm, they participated quarterly in the profitability of the firm.

5. Help team members understand their primary function is to give you the tools necessary to make it easier for your new prospects and clients to say "YES."

   Hire people who have opposite skill sets to yours. We used the Kolbe Index (www.Kolbe.com), which proved to be very accurate and useful for our group. We always wanted our staff working in their areas of strength; we did not want them trying to work on their weaknesses.

6. Make sure that team members understand their ultimate job is to free you up, so you can focus on four things:

   a. Find new relationships.

   b. Socialize/break bread with existing relationships.

   c. Get the prospects or clients to say yes.

   d. Take a lot of time off.

7. Be sure you have a well-drafted non-compete/non-solicitation agreement that all employees sign. I spent a lot of money on this, and it has saved my bacon on more than one occasion.

I'm a firm believer in the Dan Sullivan mantra that, "Time off is a prerequisite, not a reward." In the last two years I owned the business I skied more than thirty days, took the entire summer off, and wasn't at the office unless there was a reason. I could do that because I had a team motivated by the bottom line. Because of the way we compensated our people, I never had to worry about productivity. If the firm wasn't making money, it would ultimately impact each member of the team. It's not like when the "cat's away, the mice will play," because if the mice played, their compensation at the end of the quarter would be less than stellar.

The bottom line is that I positioned myself as the founder and CEO of the business. Clients understood they were buying the services of the firm, not me. They had to agree to work with various members of our team. We continually marketed the strengths of the entire group, and more importantly, we marketed our process and our philosophy of money, Lifestyle Driven Investing™.

From the day they came on board, each client was introduced to their relationship manager as well as to the other members of the team who were identified as being integral to the success of their process. All members of their team begin to interact with them from day one. In particular, it was the relationship manager's job to shepherd the client through the process. We had very specific steps in our process, and it was the relationship manager's job to ensure the standards of our process and our firm were upheld.

In the end, we tried to put ourselves in our clients' shoes. If the client thought they were buying me, what would happen to the client and their financial situation if something happened to me? If I got hit by a Mack truck, did the client have to find a new advisor? I didn't ever want the clients to rely solely upon me or any one person in our firm, not from day one and not ten years down the line.

WHERE TO START?

So, where do you begin? Find one person. Require they get all their licenses and then have them sit in on every meeting and on every phone call. Teach them how to do your asset allocations, your plans, and whatever your business requires. They should screen all your calls, and when they are trained, they should be able to take care of all the servicing issues and eventually even give advice. (Again, they need to be fully licensed to give advice.)

Then, as your business grows, if they want to be given more responsibility, they have to find and train their replacement. THAT IS THE KEY. Give them the task of creating the job description; posting the job; doing the interviews; and once the new person is hired, doing all the training. Each subsequent employee has the same responsibility if they want to move up in the organization.

When should you hire? As soon as you are able. I don't believe you can grow or be successful on your own. I was lucky that my husband believed in me; even before we could really afford to hire someone, we did. We took a chance. It turned out to be the best investment we have ever made. Hiring a full-fledged team increased the value of my business more than any other investment we have ever made.

TRANSITIONING YOUR
CLIENTS TO YOUR TEAM

So, how do you help clients who are used to working with you become comfortable working with a member of your team? They are accustomed to having you pick up the phone, meet with them, and go through their quarterly or annual portfolio reviews with them. How do you get them trained so that they are not only "okay" working with your staff but also delighted to be doing so?

The first step is to direct all servicing calls to a member of your team. The easiest thing to do from day one is to never answer your telephone. That's how we started. My assistant would answer the phone, and the client would say, "May I speak to Erin?" She would say, "Erin is in a meeting, or Erin is unavailable; may I help you?" The client would express their concern or ask their question. My assistant would say, "Well, I will go ask Erin and get right back to you with her answer. I'll try and catch her between meetings."

Sure enough my assistant would come to me, tell me what the query was, and I would recommend they do (x) instead of (y). Then my assistant would call them back and relay the message. Eventually, my assistant just answered the questions. She knew what I would say or recommend. If she was unsure, she would certainly check with me beforehand. She was fully licensed to give the answer, and the clients were normally satisfied with her answer. Occasionally, at the beginning, clients STILL wanted to hear from me, but that was rare.

The next step I took was never taking a meeting or conference call by myself. I always had a staff person with me on the call or in the meeting. If it was a conference call, I would say something like, "Suzie is going to be here taking notes, and she'll get back to you with the proper forms to execute the trades (or whatever)." In the course of the call or meeting, I very intentionally kept deferring to the staff person who was with me in the meeting.

If I happened to answer the phone by accident, and the client had some type of service request, I would put them on hold and then come back and tell them I had no idea how to handle their issue. That was the job of another team member. This is when I very intentionally got "dumb" in the business. I would imply I had no idea how to get that check cut from their account or send them that IRA distribution form. I always told them that I would ask my assistant, Joe, to take care of it immediately. In the future, instead of calling me to get an IRA distribution form, they would naturally call Joe.

When it comes to service items, like forms or check requests, you should never know the answer to, nor be able to assist with, the service issue. You should only know the answers to questions about the bigger items like investments, strategies, or other big-picture matters. Always defer to the staff person, even if you know how to send out a distribution form. At first, you may have to "pretend" you don't know how to do it; otherwise, you may continue to be asked to do things, and you will never get out of working IN your business.

In my course, I teach the three-step process for transitioning the client to a licensed member of your team. You begin with your C/D clients in the first year, where your team member learns how to overcome any objections your clients may have. This is a very low-risk way to expose your team members to the various questions and situations that come up. The next year you transition your B clients and then finally in year three, your A clients. It is a seamless process and frees up your time to focus on the highest and best use of your time.

The bottom line is: If you want to build the business of your dreams, a business that will have significant value when you are ready to exit, you have to hire, teach, and rely upon others to do practically everything. The sooner you begin that process the better.

RULES OF ENGAGEMENT

Another thing we did was create "Rules of Engagement" so there were never any questions as to how we worked. We actually called this document the "Expectations of Our Engagement," but internally we called it the ROE. This was a three-page document that acknowledged we understood they have relationships with other advisors. They have other stockbrokers, bankers, and CPAs, and each of those other advisors has a unique way of doing business with them. Some of them pick up their phone right away, some have voicemails, some have secretaries, and some return calls within twenty-four hours or the next day.

In this document, we clearly outlined how we did business. For instance, in the rules, it stated that by engaging in our services, they agreed to work with various members of our team. They agreed that they would be serviced primarily by a lead advisor and/or a relationship manager, who would guide them through the process. It was clearly laid out in the Expectations of Our Engagement document that I would know what was always going on with their case. I didn't want them to think I had completely abdicated my role in the firm. I just didn't have to be in all the meetings for the client to be well served.

The document also stated the three ways we got paid:

1. We got paid a fee for doing the plan. That fee was based on the complexity of their case and was paid up front before work began.
2. We expected to be paid on implementation of the plan through product fees, referral fees, commissions, or assets under management fees.
3. We relied on the active goodwill of our clients.

If they were happy with the service and experiences they'd had with our group, then we expected them to introduce us to their friends and associates who might need financial planning.

We were very clear in the expectations of engagement that we relied upon our current clients to introduce us to our next clients. We told them we did no national advertising, and our entire business grew through personal referrals from satisfied clients.

We also discussed our expectation that they would become renewing clients with our firm. We were not looking for one-time customers but clients who would stay with our firm for decades to come. We told them we would always strive to exceed their expectations and asked for permission to check in with them every twelve to eighteen months for honest feedback as to how we were doing. We set up the expectations for future meetings ahead of time, telling them we would ask them to give us a grade on a scale of 1 to 10 on how we were doing. If it was anything other than a 10, we wanted constructive feedback as to what we could do to get that score to a 10. We were also clear with every engagement that we did not do any "transactional business." A prospect could not come to us and say, "What would you do with $1 million?" Unless they hired and paid us a fee to create a financial plan, we would take a pass. While we preferred to engage clients by doing a comprehensive financial plan, including a review of their estate planning documents, etc., we also had a second tier of engagement called an "Investment Only" plan. From a liability standpoint, I would *urge all* advisors to have a policy wherein you protect yourself from making investment recommendations without really knowing your prospect's entire financial situation. Since litigation is so rampant, I can't emphasize this strongly enough.

Finally, make sure to set out the expectations of engagement in advance. This is the best way to ensure that clients clearly understand the relationship so there are no misunderstandings.

For more information and additional resources, go to www.erinbotsford.com.

QUESTIONS TO PONDER:

- **Have you reached the limit of where you can grow your business on your own?**

  There are limits to what one person can do in growing a business. If you've reached that limit, and even if you haven't, it's probably time to hire other people to work for you. You cannot grow a business that runs without your day-to-day involvement if you have to be involved in every aspect of client engagement.

- **How can you build the best possible team?**

  Hire people to do the technical work first. Your goal is to train one person and then have them train the second, third, and fourth employees. Be sure you have a well-drafted non-compete/non-solicitation agreement that all employees sign.

- **Are you ready to transition from salesperson to business owner?**

  Once you've built the team, it's time to leverage your team members by creating an environment where the client is served without you being involved in every step of the process. After a period of transition, the best thing you can do is intentionally hand off your credibility to your team members. Highlighting your team member's credentials and overtly telling clients how valuable that team member is to your firm goes a long way in easing a client's mind about working with someone other than you.

- **Have you developed your own "rules of engagement" for your business?**

It's certainly worth your time and energy to set expectations about how you have organized your business, including a section outlining your role in the business versus the roles of your team members with whom the clients will work. We were very up-front in our initial meeting that all clients must agree to work with various members of our team. The ROE also laid out how we got paid, our expectations for client referrals, how customers could deliver feedback, and so on. It sets the stage for your relationship with the new clients and prevents misunderstandings later on.

CHAPTER 7

USING SYSTEMS AND PROCESSES TO CREATE RAVING FANS

T he right systems and processes—and vigilance about maintaining them—are *essential* if you want to grow a large practice that doesn't depend on you. The more things are systematized, the less chance things will fall through the cracks and the greater the likelihood clients will have a consistently superior experience with your firm.

SUPERIOR AND CONSISTENT CUSTOMER EXPERIENCE

We created every system and process in our firm with the client experience in mind. Consumers are heavily influenced by the experiences they have as they make a purchase. Nordstrom knows this. Nordstrom customers know that if they need to return something today or next year, they will have a similar experience, a transaction with no questions asked. Interestingly enough, consumers and clients are also creatures of habit. If they liked the experience, they want to have that experience repeated over and over and over again. Changes to the experience, whether good or bad, can alter the way a client perceives your business.

By way of analogy, consider the habitual nature of people who go to church. They tend to sit in the same section of the church each week, in the same pew, and usually around the same people, because they want consistency of experience. One of the reasons McDonald's is so successful is that people can go to a McDonald's anywhere in the world—whether it is in Alamogordo, New Mexico; New York City; or Munich, Germany—and have a very predictable experience. The cheeseburger will be warm or hot, and it will taste virtually the same as the last one they had, no matter where it was consumed.

The same principles apply to our business. It is important to create systems and processes to (1) define the experience you want your clients to have and (2) assure that the experience is repeated over and over again. You don't want your clients calling or coming in each time and having a different experience; it really changes the nature of their relationship with you.

How do you do this in practical terms? Here are some examples. Make sure every team member answers the phone the same way. Set up the conference room in exactly the same manner every time. Greet customers in the same way, regardless of which staff member is giving the greeting. If you know your clients' drink preferences ahead of time, serve them their drink of choice without them having to ask.

Clients are likely to sit in the same seat in your conference room each time they enter. We liked to control where the clients sat the first time they come in because we knew they would gravitate to that same seat the next time they come. Therefore, we had a system that determined where we wanted them to be seated the first time they entered our office so that we could optimize their experience with us.

If there was a husband and wife, we always sat the woman at the head of the table and her husband on the side that did not face the door of the conference room. Why? One, because we wanted her to feel like she had equal control in the meeting and to see herself as someone who had something vital to contribute to the discussion. Two, we did not want the male client distracted by anything going on in the hallway outside the conference room. Since we had glass windows, we tried to keep the distractions to a minimum.

Often the woman will not readily accept the seat at the head of the table. So, I explained to her it was much easier on me to have her seated at the head and her husband directly across from me, so I didn't end up with "tennis head," turning my head from side to side if they were on opposite sides of the table. That usually worked. Another tactic is to make sure the receptionist serves her drink at the head of the table so she knows that spot was prepared for her. The extent you create consistent experiences will be the extent to which your clients feel comfortable coming in and referring others to you.

SYSTEMS CONSTANTLY EVOLVE

We had hundreds of systems and processes, but it took decades to come up with all of them. Obviously, as we changed brokers/

dealers, moved, hired new positions, etc., over the years, we had to refresh our systems. It's like cleaning the rooms of your house. By the time you clean the last room in your house, the first one you went through needs to be re-cleaned. I'll go through a couple of systems we established so you can see the ones we consider the most important.

A SAMPLING OF OUR SYSTEMS
CLIENT MEETING AGENDAS

We created a written agenda for every meeting, beginning with the first official meeting we had with the client. More than anything, the agenda was for our benefit, so we (1) remembered everything we needed to discuss with the client and (2) had backup evidence for the file that covered what we discussed in the meeting. The client's version of the agenda only showed broad categories and provided space for taking notes. The advisor's version of the agenda had detailed notes from prior calls, meetings, and/or discussions to remind the advisor of important details he or she may not recall. For instance, the advisor's copy would likely have the names and ages of all family members. There might even be notes on personal information the client has shared, such as whether there was a new baby in the family, an impending retirement or a vacation, or the death of a dog—whatever was important to the client. It strikes an amazing chord with the client when you make mention of something that is vitally important to them. Of course, there is no way any of our advisors could recall all those details for all their clients. The only way you can do this effectively is to create a system to serve as your memory.

In the first couple of meetings, the agenda might be three pages long, because we had a lot to cover. We discussed the client's risk management profile, their current estate planning documents, and their balance sheet, and spent time reviewing investments and insurance, etc. We wanted to be sure the advisor was set up for success and didn't come out of the meeting without covering all the important items with the client. The agenda kept the meeting very focused. Anything that wasn't covered in the current meeting would be moved to the next agenda.

CLIENT SEATING SYSTEM

As mentioned earlier, consistency of experience was of utmost importance to us. Therefore, our conference rooms were always set up with water and a writing tablet with a pen at each seat. And, to repeat what I said earlier, if it was a husband and wife, we sat the wife at the head of the table and had the husband seated on the side of the table where he would face the least number of potential distractions.

TWO-MINUTE WARNING SYSTEM

We had our "two-minute warning" system for arriving clients. We had a bell that rang in the back of the office when the front door opened. We instituted this before we had an official receptionist sitting up front, and it served us, especially if the receptionist was away from his or her desk. (Our receptionist was often my assistant or the assistant to other advisors, so he or she was often seated out of sight of the front door.) Once that bell rang, we expected someone to greet our guests within two minutes or less and lead them into one of our conference rooms. We don't want clients sitting in our waiting room without having been greeted. (Ideally, we didn't want them sitting in our reception area chairs at all.) It was office policy that every person on the team had to be listening for that door. If the receptionist was on the phone or in the restroom, it was up to another team member to get to the front door within two minutes to greet our guest. Eventually, we were able to get a Ring doorbell so team members could see on their phones who was coming in the front door.

Whoever greeted the guests escorted them to the appropriate conference room and would also take their drink order. If they were already our clients, we kept track of their drink preferences. As the receptionist seated them, she would typically say something like, "Would you like a Diet Coke?" or, "I see you take black coffee," or "Do you still take your coffee with cream and two sugars?" Clients love it when you remember them and their drink preferences. We wanted the environment in our office to be more like *Cheers*, where everybody knows your name. It was also our policy that the clients were never left alone in the conference room. A staff member introduced our Founder's Video (which I highly recommend you have) and then that team member stayed in the room and chatted with the client until the advisor or relationship manager arrived.

THE RITZ-CARLTON EXPERIENCE

As a part of our training, we sent several members of our team to the Ritz-Carlton Experience training. The information, systems, and techniques they brought back to share with the group were invaluable. We adopted many of the tools used by The Ritz-Carlton. For instance, we had Monday morning meetings each week, similar to The Ritz-Carlton "lineup," where one member of our team shared an inspirational quote or delivered a positive message. We recognized "atta girls" or "atta boys" among the team for great performances the previous week.

We had a Botsford credo and a list of twelve service values that we lived by. We tried to instill the idea that we were "ladies and gentlemen serving ladies and gentlemen," just as they train employees to do at The Ritz-Carlton. Most importantly, everything we did was filtered through a corporate lens that asked the question, "How would The Ritz-Carlton do this?" For instance, when we served our clients lunch, it was on nice china with cloth napkins. We served water or soft drinks in nice glasses versus in cans, plastic bottles, or paper cups. We even had a signature scent in the office, so it was familiar each time clients entered. As time went on, we adapted and evolved our process. Where we used to just have traditional pens and paper in the conference room, we had pens with a stylus on the end in case our clients wanted to take notes on their iPad or iPhone.

WHO WILL DO WHAT BY WHEN?

At the end of a meeting, we always wanted the clients to know who would do what by when. We never wanted the clients to leave the meeting without knowing what the next steps were. We wanted them to know that we would contact them next and when that would be, or that the ball was in their court, and we expected a call back from them. Generally, we wouldn't leave the ball in their court. We liked to control the contact, so most often we'd schedule the next meeting or call right then, while we had them in front of us. If the clients left the office and it was not clear who would do what by when, the relationship manager would send an e-mail outlining the next steps.

DOWNLOAD SYSTEM

Another system we relied on, to make sure we typed up a good and accurate synopsis of every call and every meeting, was the "Download System." Each relationship manager was responsible for providing a very thorough download of everything that happened in the meeting or on the call. Sometimes our relationship managers liked to type their downloads; some liked to use a transcription service such as Words Express. Some of the relationship managers took copious notes on their iPad in iNotes. Regardless, the office policy was that within twenty-four hours, all meetings and calls that had taken place would be downloaded into our customer relationship management (CRM) system and become a part of the client's permanent record.

We adopted a uniform format for our downloads. The first part of the download listed who was in the meeting. The next section contained all the tasks to be completed. Some of those tasks were immediately assigned to others on the team to be completed. The relationship manager completed some follow-ups, but all were outlined in the download. The third part of the download provided a clear description of what took place in the meeting and any decisions that were made (i.e., like the minutes taken at any meeting). If there were investment products discussed, the download also included any disclosures that were made regarding things like liquidity features, risks, fees, and charges for the product, etc. The relationship manager could also use his or her download to help create the next meeting agenda. It was a body of notes that captured the essence of every call or meeting.

DAILY PHONE LOGS

Another system we used was our "daily phone logs." The daily phone log was a record of every call and/or servicing issue that took place and any e-mail that came in or went out. All of this was posted to the client record. Early on, the staff would create a Word document and pass it around. At the end of the day, they would either e-mail or fax it to me wherever I was, so I could see what happened during the day. Technology certainly allowed us to evolve. Eventually, all the downloads ended up in the client's permanent CRM record, and at exactly 5:01 p.m. a report was generated that outlined all e-mails and all calls that came in or out of the office. Everyone on the team had access to these phone logs in case they wanted to know what happened on a given day. Regardless of where I was in the world, I could review everything that had happened on any given day.

ANSWERING THE PHONE—
GREETING THE CLIENT

We tried not to use voicemail. We tried to catch the phone by the second ring. I hate voicemail and think it's very impersonal, so we wanted our clients or prospects to be able to talk to an individual. In addition, we had a policy that we returned all phone calls on the same day. We also had a policy wherein a client was always referred to as Mr. and/or Mrs. until they had specifically asked to be called by their first names. Even if they gave permission for one person on the team to call them by their first name, that did not imply any other team members had the authority to refer to them by their first name. Each member of the team had to be personally invited to call a client by his or her first name.

COVERING FOR TEAM MEMBERS

We required everybody to have access to everyone else's business e-mail. Hence, we asked our team members not to use their Botsford Group e-mail for personal business. This allowed for ease in backing up team members when they were in meetings or out of the office. As often as possible, whoever served as the backup, checked the colleague's e-mails. If they saw an e-mail come in from a client, we wanted to immediately respond to the client and say something like, "Mr. Smith, I see that you've sent Joe an e-mail. Joe is in a meeting right now, but I'll be sure he gets your message or e-mail and responds to you in a timely manner." Clients want to be acknowledged. They don't necessarily need to have their issue resolved or question answered immediately, but they want to make sure their e-mail was received, or their phone message was acknowledged. To the greatest extent possible, we were pretty fast on the draw, and we tried to get back to them as quickly as possible.

BIRTHDAY ACKNOWLEDGMENT SYSTEM

We thought it was very important to acknowledge our clients' birthdays. It was the one day each year that we could honor them with a phone call and a birthday card. We had a process for each.

Birthday cards

Every month, one of our employees would download a list from our CRM system identifying clients who had birthdays for that month. She handwrote the envelope and placed a real stamp on the envelope. About three to five days before our client's birthday, the card was mailed.

Birthday calls

One of the first e-mails generated each day by one of our employees was a list of all birthdays for that day AND for the next day. It was our policy that all clients were called on their birthdays by their assigned relationship manager before 10:00 a.m.

Another system we began using was the "Birthday Lunch." We got a list of all the birthdays for the month, and the relationship manager chose which of his or her clients to take to lunch. We usually picked clients we enjoyed spending time with and those we would like to replicate. It was always fun to work with the friends and associates of our best clients.

At one point, we began focusing on clients who were not as close to us on a personal level, and it completely changed the nature of our relationship with those clients. It was amazing to see what a meal honoring a client's birthday can do! To make this happen, one of the assistants made a call to schedule the lunch. As a present, we ordered a *Time* or *Life* magazine that was published in the week of their birth. The magazines can be purchased at www.papermags.com. The clients have LOVED getting a real magazine in its original condition that was published in the year of their birth. We received a lot of great feedback on that, in addition to a lot of goodwill and referrals. Our referrals almost doubled once we started the birthday lunches with the magazines.

CLIENT BROCHURE ASSEMBLY PROCESS

We had a written system for things like the client brochure assembly process. This system outlined what marketing materials went into our marketing packets, down to the order of the piece and whether they were placed on the right side or left side of the folder.

TIFFANY WINE GLASS REFERRAL PROCESS

Each new client who contracted with us was sent a classic Tiffany wine glass they could use to drink wine or their morning juice. This was a small token of our appreciation for their business. In a letter we sent with the glass, we let them know that we had also sent the same type of glass to the person who referred them to us. Sometimes we sent Tiffany wine glasses to several people: anyone who mentioned us to them or had any influence in their decision to hire us. We also outlined our Tiffany wine glass program in this initial letter and hoped that, during the course of our relationship, they would collect many wine glasses by referring many people to us.

I know this seems ridiculous, but the Tiffany wine glass program was a huge success. I once had a client who seemed to call every Monday to give me the names of new prospects I should call that week. My response was always, "Dennis, you must have had a party this weekend and broken a few glasses!" It always made for a good laugh. Once a client had received twelve classic red wine glasses, we moved to white wine, champagne, and even tea glasses. Fortunately, we have had clients who have sent us so many clients over the decades that we have been able to stock their china cabinets with beautiful glasses. In your area, if Tiffany glasses are not available or too expensive, Riedel wine glasses are a great substitute.

NEW CLIENT ONBOARDING CHECKLIST

From the time a client engaged with us, we employed a checklist and a process for our initial engagement with them. For instance, the minute the contracting paperwork came in, an e-mail went to the client acknowledging receipt of their check and introducing them to their new team. In addition, clients were given a copy of the Steps of our Process, so they knew where they were in the planning process. As soon as that e-mail went out, the assigned team followed up with the new client to be sure they had their contact information. Each step of the process was well defined for maximum efficiency.

REFERRAL THANK-YOU PROCESS

Any time we heard that our clients were talking about us, we wanted to acknowledge their efforts on our behalf. We hand-wrote thank-you notes for all referrals, regardless of whether the referral became a client. In addition, our clients would receive a small gift in the mail (usually, it was some form of candy or cookie, but it could be golf balls or whatever that particular client was interested in).

CREATING SYSTEMS IS TIME WELL SPENT

These are just a few of the systems and processes we used. It is important to note that I always knew having written systems and processes would be significant; I just couldn't find the time to sit still long enough to map them out and write them down. Eventually (and unfortunately) I was forced to do so in the early 2000s. At the time, we were a very small team, with less than five of us.

My personal assistant's husband was diagnosed with and eventually died of brain cancer. Through no fault of her own, my assistant was out of the office on a very frequent basis to go with her husband to doctor's appointments and attend to his needs in his final days on this earth. Finally, she stayed home with him full-time for the last four months of his life, which left us with a gaping hole in our office.

My assistant knew how to do everything. She was a wizard when it came to making things happen. Unfortunately, all that information was in her head, which didn't do me any good when she was out. As she sat with her husband as he slept, I asked her to start typing up everything she did from the time she walked in the door until the end of the day. I continued to pay her even though she was out, so she was very willing to help us in any way she could. I told her I needed her to write down everything she did in such detail that a monkey could do it.

Eventually, I hired a male temp and one by one, I asked him if he could follow the systems she had listed. For instance, for the birthday card process, I asked her to get into her own head and type out: "This is how I figure out which clients are having birthdays. I go to the CRM program, I enter the field I am looking for, I print out this field, and I type up a list. Then I go to '*X*' website and order the birthday cards. When they come in, I do '*Y*.' This is where I order stamps; this is where I keep the stamps. This is how I address the cards. There is a box on my desk with the days of the months on it. After I address the envelopes, I put the cards in the slot of the date that is five days ahead of the client's birthday. Each morning I pull out the cards to be mailed, etc."

It was an arduous process to say the least, but we got twenty or thirty systems created during that awful time in her life. She said it was a godsend having something to think about, and it was certainly a godsend for us.

After that, we just had to improve on the systems we already had in place and create new systems for new things we wanted to do. One thing I adopted was as part of any new employee's quarterly bonus compensation, they had to proactively update our systems and process manual. It was a way for them to learn our business AND a way I was able to keep our systems current. I hope you can create your own systems and processes before you have to. Let me assure you, being proactive is a better way to go.

For more information and additional resources, go to www. erinbotsford.com.

QUESTIONS TO PONDER:

- **Have you created systems and processes at your business so that everything is streamlined and consistent for every client?**

  Consider applying systems to meetings, client seating, greeting clients, customer service, assigning responsibility for post-meeting tasks, case notes, phones, e-mails, client onboarding, and client birthdays.

- **Which systems and processes should you document?**

  If you are having trouble getting started on this, just start asking questions. Questions like: "How, specifically, do we greet clients? How do we seat clients in the conference room? How do we send birthday cards? What is our system for sending out IRA distributions?" Every question that comes up indicates there is a process that should or could be documented.

- **When did you last review your current systems to see which ones could be scrapped or needed to be refreshed?**

  If something's not working well for your clients, then it may be time to rework your existing systems so that nothing falls through the cracks.

CHAPTER 8

PSYCHOLOGY AND
PERSONAL DISCIPLINE

I f I could change one thing about the training program I went
through at my first broker/dealer, I'd make sure there were
classes on the psychology of sales. In fact, there were many times
I wish I'd gotten my degree in psychology instead of business,
because so much of what we do involves psychology.

Consider this: The quintessential task of a financial advisor is
to identify a path for the client to follow. We create a plan. It
usually involves purchasing investment or insurance products.
Sometimes it involves working with other advisors like CPAs or
attorneys. We all know the plan isn't worth the paper it is written
on if the client doesn't take action. We also know clients don't
always take action or agree with our plan. Why? We think we created a perfectly good plan that will lead to the exact outcome the
client has articulated. Why doesn't the client just go along with it?
That is the $64,000 question.

In my career, I have more than once literally scratched my
head and asked myself, "What happened? How did I get this so

wrong?" I have learned over time that there are a number of key concepts to understand:

1. Prospects often have preconceived ideas of who you are and what you do. In order to differentiate yourself from your competitors, you have to quickly change any preconceived notions; otherwise, you look just like the last advisor with whom they met.

2. Clients may not be able to articulate what they truly want from you.

3. Clients don't necessarily want your best answer immediately; they tend to appreciate it when you walk them through the process so they can arrive at the same conclusion you have.

4. Women approach financial services with different expectations and needs than men do. Therefore, you have to approach women differently.

5. If you want to win over both members of a couple, you have to show how a plan meets both of their needs.

6. Don't ignore or patronize the female partner in a couple.

7. If you are a female advisor who works with male clients, be careful not to intimidate the man's partner.

8. Don't use language that's too advanced for your prospects or clients.

THE PRECONCEIVED NOTIONS OF PROSPECTS

The first thing I always teach advisors when I am coaching them is this: When a new prospective client walks in the door, he or she likely has a preconceived notion about who you are and what you do, largely based on the last person they met who called themselves a financial advisor. For some prospects, their only experience has been with a stockbroker, so they think you'll be just like the last stockbroker they met. Some have only dealt with life insurance agents, so they assume that you're going to be just like the last life insurance agent they met. Unfortunately, this is likely true for everyone in our industry. People often have preconceived notions, not only about who we are but also about how we think and what we'll likely recommend for them. The first thing you have to change, as quickly as possible, is that perception.

Also keep in mind, most people maintain the perception that someone who holds a juris doctorate (an attorney) is extremely smart and therefore held in the highest regard. After the attorney, someone who holds the title of CPA (certified public accountant), is often considered the second most credible advisor. I always joke that the next person in the credibility pecking order is probably the Mercedes dealer, followed by us, their financial advisor.

As I mentioned in my introduction, some of this perception arises from the actual barriers to entry in each of those professions. The attorney, whom clients or prospects hold in the highest regard, has gone through college and law school and has passed the bar exam. The CPA has gone through college, perhaps gotten a master's degree, and sat for the CPA exam. The Mercedes dealer? We don't know how much schooling he's had. The financial advisor, other than taking the Series 7 test and maybe the Series 63 or 65, hasn't had to clear the same hurdles as the attorney or the CPA, so it stands to reason why prospects might regard us as "less than" their other professional advisors. The first thing we have to do is prove to prospective clients in a short period of time why we deserve to be given the same credence as their most trusted advisor(s).

CLIENT PSYCHOLOGY 101: UNDERSTANDING WHAT YOUR PROSPECTIVE CLIENT TRULY WANTS

What does your prospective client REALLY want? That can be a very tough question. Sometimes what they tell you they want is not what they really want. Sometimes they don't know what they really want. Other times, what they want isn't available in the real world. Have you ever had someone tell you they were VERY risk averse, but they also wanted to beat the S&P 500? I've had people say they wanted to beat the S&P 500 but to make sure their principal was guaranteed and completely liquid.

In my firm, I worked mostly with retirees, people who were age fifty-five and older, who had worked for thirty-five to forty years. I had to learn to read between the lines and interpret what they really wanted. I learned that, for the most part, my clients wanted to be able to do what they wanted, when they wanted, with whom they wanted, and not worry about their money. The degree to which I could help them not worry about their money was the degree to which they would either hire me (if they were a prospect) or keep me (if they were a client).

On the other hand, your target market might be accumulators who are willing to take a little more risk. They want accelerated rates of return. They have an entirely different mindset, so if you start talking to the accumulators about something as boring as bonds that don't represent accelerated growth, you'll lose them.

I'm firmly convinced that if you want to be successful in your business you really have to understand the mindset of the person sitting in front of you. At the end of the day, your job is to get the client to say "yes" to your recommendations. Presumably, your recommendations are the precise prescription to get the clients to the place they told you they wanted to go. To get there, they need to take action. It is your job to help move them along that path. As such, they NEED you to read between the lines of what they are saying and what they are not saying. They NEED you to figure out what makes them tick. They NEED you to figure out what they are afraid of, because they are likely not going to tell you. The extent to which you can understand their psyche is the extent to which they will say "yes," and you will become their trusted advisor.

A COUNTERINTUITIVE WAY TO GAIN CLIENTS' TRUST

I had been in business for over twenty years, yet I missed something that eventually came back to haunt me. From about 1995 until 2008, I was fortunate to work with a group of executives from one Fortune 500 company who were all connected to one another and also very good referrers. The phone would ring and the new prospect would say, "My friend Joe says I should work with you." The strength of those warm referrals cannot be overstated. With a strong referral, generally the new client believes your advice to them will be similar to the advice you gave to their friend. Often, when you get a warm referral, there is very little pushback when it comes to product implementation.

Unfortunately, these clients were in Atlanta, and I lived in Dallas. After thirteen years of commuting between the two cities, I decided in 2008 to stop traveling as much and to build a network of new clients in the Dallas area. These were all brand-new prospects, and I did not have the benefit of trust that comes with a warm referral. But I didn't realize that at first. I used the identical process for these new clients and expected to get the same results. Because my advice was sound and ideally suited to these new clients, I was befuddled as to why the first couple of new clients gave me so much pushback when it came to implementing the investment products.

I knew something was wrong, but I couldn't put my finger on it. I finally decided to ask one of these new clients, a woman who had also become a good friend to me. My client (I'll call her Susan) had been in both the commercial and residential real estate business for her entire thirty-year career. She had gone through our financial planning process, and when I asked her why she and other new clients hesitated to implement my firm's recommendations, she was able to immediately articulate the reason. In fact, she said, "I know exactly why this is happening!" What she said was eye-opening.

She gave me this analogy: "Erin, when I was new to the commercial real estate business, people would call up from all parts of the country and describe to me over the phone the type of commercial real estate space they needed. They would say they needed fifty thousand square feet and wanted a downtown location with this amenity or that. By the time I got off the phone, I knew exactly the right space for them. After all, I was a professional and I knew every property that existed in the Dallas area. The representatives from the company would fly in, and I would take them to the space I had in mind. Every time, they were astounded at the degree to which this space matched exactly what they had told me over the phone. They were excited and, by all indications, they were interested in leasing the space I showed them. But then they'd get on the plane and with very few exceptions, they would get 'buyer's remorse' or start wavering in their decision to lease the space."

Susan said it took her a while to figure out what was going on. She could commiserate with me because I was experiencing the same thing. I knew exactly the right investment recommendations to make for each new client, just as I had known the exact formula for all the warm referrals who had come over the years. But these new people, who didn't come from a warm source, were hesitant to take my advice. In fact, I lost three in a row. Why?

Susan then proceeded to tell me what she learned and how it applied to what I was experiencing. She said, "Erin, let's use the example of residential real estate. When I was in that market, my greatest desire was to find my buyers the perfect house for them as quickly as possible. If I could spare making them look at twenty houses and only have to look at two, I thought I was doing them a favor. So, I would work very hard and try to select the perfect houses for them; I could drive them directly to what I felt were the one or two that were best suited for them. Each and every time, the buyers agreed I had nailed it. My expectation would be that they would sign a purchase agreement, and we'd be in escrow within a few days. But each and every time, the buyers would get buyer's remorse. Why? Because although buyers trusted me, they wanted to ensure *themselves* they had seen every single home that remotely met their specifications.

"In their minds, they would say, 'I know Susan showed us two properties that were amazing and completely met our requirements, but could there be other homes that were even more right or more amazing for us?'"

The same held true for Susan with her commercial real estate clients. The company representatives felt responsible as agents for their firms to make sure they had seen ALL the office buildings that could have met the company's needs, not just the ones Susan showed them. Here's how Susan relayed her experience as a client with us. She said, "Erin, when my husband and I engaged your firm, I'm sure you knew by the time we left your office the first time the exact investments you were going to recommend for us. You are a seasoned professional, and you know what our situation required. But here's the problem: We didn't know. Just like the people who want to drive around and see every house that meets their real estate requirements, we wanted to 'drive around' and see all the potential investment products that could meet our requirements. In a sense, you went right to the first house—the perfect house for us—but you didn't give us the chance to drive around and see all the other houses so we could see for ourselves how perfect your recommendations were."

I was never so grateful to anyone. As a result, I created an entire process based on the idea of driving my clients around to see every investment so they could be a part of the process of narrowing down the final recommendations. We called this part of our process our "Investment Collaboration" process. We had an entire meeting dedicated to going through all the various types of investments that are out there—in broad general categories—and giving our clients the chance to learn, provide feedback, and be a part of the overall *collaborative* process. We found this collaborative method gave the clients a sense of ownership in the final outcome presented in the plan. In the end, we normally arrived at the same place we would have gotten to without this meeting, but this process gave our clients the confidence that comes from knowing they had reviewed the alternatives themselves and come to the same conclusion as their advisor.

THE PSYCHOLOGY OF WORKING WITH WOMEN

If you are working with a married couple, the biggest mistake you can make as a financial advisor is to discount, marginalize, ignore, or talk down to the wife. It is a HUGE mistake, but one I see repeatedly. Having coached many financial advisors on this issue, I have concluded that most people in the industry are clueless as to how to deal with female clients. You might think this is only a problem when the client is a single woman. That couldn't be further from the truth. The bigger issue is how women who are part of a couple are treated. To me, this shows a complete lack of understanding as to who the actual decision-maker likely is in the relationship.

What you should never forget is that it is the woman, in almost every case, who makes all the decisions! That comes as a surprise, doesn't it? Okay, I'll soften my stance just a bit: *It is the woman who retains what I call "ABSOLUTE VETO POWER!"* You never want her to exercise her superpower!

I'll give you a personal example. Many years ago, my husband, Bob, and I built a house and decided to put a pool in the backyard. Bob called me one day and said the gentleman who was building our pool wanted to meet with both of us to talk about the number and type of pumps that would be required for our pool. I immediately said, "No honey, you can handle that; I'm not really interested in dealing with that subject. Whatever you decide is fine with me." But my husband said, "No, this man really insists you be there for the meeting; he wants to talk to both of us." Reluctantly, I agreed and made a point of leaving my office at 3:30 p.m. so I could attend the meeting.

At precisely 4:00 p.m., the gentleman arrived and spent ninety minutes talking to us about pool pumps. The problem was he never once looked at me or acknowledged I was even in the room. It was so unbelievably rude. I was furious! Believe it or not, I didn't say anything. I sat there and thought, "I think I'm supposed to learn something." The meeting ended. We showed him to the door. I shook his hand and was very kind, but as soon as he left, I looked at my husband, swiped my right hand under my neck as if to cut it off and said: "Nope, that's not going to happen. We are not buying anything from that man." My husband looked at me incredulously and said, "Are you kidding? The man just spent an hour and a half with us; he has a great product." I said I didn't care if he had spent half his life with us. He was condescending; he ignored me entirely, especially after insisting I attend the meeting. There was no way I was going to reward that behavior by giving him his next sale and that was the end of it. VETO!

From my perspective, there's absolutely no question about who runs the show, or at the very least, who has absolute veto power in a couple. The degree to which you acknowledge that reality is the degree to which you'll be successful in winning with couples. This shouldn't come as a shock. Our society recognizes the power women hold, something that is even acknowledged in a few adages, such as, "If mama ain't happy, ain't nobody happy." Funny as it may be, I remember what my husband told my son when he got married: "Son, the only two words you need to learn to have a successful marriage are, 'Yes, dear.'"

Here are some other pointers that might be helpful to know regarding the woman in a couple. As much as a woman says she doesn't want to be at the meeting, sometimes she really does want to be there. Either way, you have to make the woman feel like she is a valued part of the process. You have to engage her on the heart level, not just the numbers level. I told the wife I very much appreciated her coming to the meeting, and as I have said before, I seated her at the head of the table. I told her that her input was incredibly valuable; something that was, in fact, underscored by where she was positioned at the table. If we were doing estate planning, I told her

I would not conduct that particular meeting unless she was present. I really went out of my way to make her want to be there and be an active participant. I also told both of them I didn't expect them to learn everything I knew. I told them they would probably only remember ten percent of what we talked about, but what I did want was for *both of them* to leave with a sense of confidence that we knew what we were doing, that we would listen intently to what each of them had to say, and that we would do our best to respect their time. I stressed to her how grateful I was that she cared about their outcome and, as a result, I would do my best to deliver the best possible solutions.

Because I'm a woman advisor who worked with couples, I also faced another challenge: Sometimes women prospects can be a little intimidated by another woman. I don't know why that is, but I have observed this on enough occasions to know it merits mention. In my experience, this mostly happens with women who have chosen to stay home and raise their families. I highly respect that as the most difficult of all careers, but the woman may not know me or know I feel that way. If you are a female advisor and you sense this "tension," there is a simple thing you can do to help the woman in the couple feel completely at ease with you.

Make it a point to focus on the woman at the beginning of the meeting. Give her almost all your attention, while giving her husband just a glance now and then. Keep focusing on her until you sense the barrier has melted. That is what I did. I went out of my way and overtly gave the woman nearly one hundred percent of my attention until I had her nodding her head in agreement with me. When I knew she and I were on the same page and that she not only didn't feel threatened by me but also came to believe I had her best interests at heart, then I would bring her husband into the conversation. Until that time, my attention was on her.

I suggest male advisors take the same approach. Seat the woman at the head of the table and engage her from the very beginning.

Even if she shrinks back and lets her husband do most or all of the talking, stay aware of her presence at the table and keep her engaged in all parts of the discussion. Treat her in a way that lets her know that you understand she is ultimately in charge of the meeting's outcome, because in all likelihood she is. I can assure you that before the garage door opens on their return trip home, she will have her say about whether or not you will be the couple's next advisor.

The other thing I did—when I sensed that the wife (or in some cases, the husband) didn't have much knowledge of financial planning—was to speak at the level of the lowest understanding in the room. In any meeting where we would be discussing industry concepts, I would always preface my comments by telling those present I was going to be speaking at a fifth-grade level. I told them I was not doing this to be insulting or patronizing; I just wanted to be sure everyone in the room was on the same page and was tracking with me. As soon as I could see they were with me, then I would raise the level of how I spoke to them. As such, I was never condescending, but I also didn't want to talk over anyone's head. Talking over someone's head does nothing to impress them. You just lose them and the opportunity to get the outcome that is best for your client. Be aware, of course, that it is not always the woman in the couple who has less financial knowledge. I have

worked with many high-powered female executives whose hus-
bands were the less-knowledgeable parties.

WHAT WOMEN WANT

If you want to get a better handle on what women want from
financial planning, consider these surprising findings from a
study done by Allianz. This European financial firm found that
forty-nine percent of women—"across all corners of life and
affluence"—fear ending up broke and homeless. What is truly
stunning is that this "irrational fear" (Allianz's term; not mine)
is found among the twenty-seven percent of women with annual
household incomes above $200,000![4]

According to the survey, the statement, "Deep down, I have
a fear of becoming a bag lady," holds true for fifty-six percent of
single women, forty-three percent of married women, fifty-four
percent of divorced women, and forty-seven percent of widowed
women.[5] It's also true for nearly half (forty-six percent) of women
Allianz considers "financially savvy and financially empowered,"[6]

4.   Allianz Life Insurance Company, "The Allianz Women, Money, and Power Study:
     Empowered and Underserved – Insight 5: 'Bag Lady' Fears Persist Among Even
     the Most Successful Women," accessed July 22, 2016, https://www.allianzlife.
     com/-/media/files/allianz/documents/ent_1462_n.pdf.

5.   Allianz Life Insurance Company, "Insight 5: 'Bag Lady' Fears Persist."

6.   Allianz Life Insurance Company, "The Allianz Women, Money, and Power Study:
     Empowered and Underserved – Insight 2: The Rise of 'Women of Influence,'"
     accessed July 22, 2016, https://www.allianzlife.com/-/media/files/allianz/docu-
     ments/ent_1462_n.pdf.

even though these women are "generally less worried about their retirement savings."[7]

Given the findings, you can assume a typical woman never wants to be placed in a situation where she feels that something could go wrong with her finances or that the rug could be pulled out from under her.

Women are generally not huge risk-takers. If they are going to take risks, they want the risk/reward profile to be well articulated.

They want to know the downside of any plan presented to them. I've noticed that very few women are comfortable rolling the dice when it comes to their investments. That said, women tend to make very good investors. They do their homework, and their expectations tend to be very realistic. They're not looking for home runs.

Single women, especially, tend to make very good investment decisions. Because they are alone, they don't have a safety net. They know it's up to them, so they usually do their research. Once they set their minds on a strategy, they tend not to second-guess it.

I wish I could say the same about widows. As a female financial advisor, I found it can be challenging working with widows. The widows we encountered in my firm were usually over sixty-five years old. Most had played a traditional role in their marriage. Typically, the husband was the primary income provider and the one who took care of their investment decisions.

A widow who came from these circumstances would often

---

7.   Allianz Life Insurance Company, "Insight 5: 'Bag Lady' Fears Persist."

bring in one of her sons, who then acted as the decision-maker. If not, she often went back to her husband's financial advisor, typically a man. I can understand this. She has always had a man managing her money and finances, so it probably gave her comfort to continue this pattern. If you look at this dynamic from a psychological standpoint, male advisors have an edge with this clientele. If I were a male advisor, I would certainly consider older widows as a potential target market.

I have had male advisors ask me if I think it is a mistake for them to go after the female market. I say, "Absolutely not." I think male advisors have a great advantage when it comes to women clients. There is already a belief that the financial world is dominated by men (which is true), so it is not so far-fetched that many women would assume a male advisor would likely have more of an aptitude for finance. The biggest thing any advisor who works with women must remember is to never talk down to a woman or worse, ignore her. Make sure her concerns are addressed and she is made to feel like an integral part of your process. If she has a spouse or partner, treat her and her partner as equals.

A NURTURING NATURE

Finally, let me admit I took advantage of the fact that I *was* a female advisor. As a female, it was assumed I have a nurturing nature. That very much appeals to women prospects and clients. With all clients, I spent an entire appointment letting them talk about themselves. Who doesn't like to talk about themselves? I asked probing questions. I wanted to know all about their family of origin, where they were raised, and what they were taught about money. I wanted to know all about their parents, siblings, nieces, and nephews.

We called this meeting our Visions and Values Conversation™. It was an opportunity for prospects and clients to talk about what's important to them. I told them I was looking for one of two things: potential "train wrecks," or opportunities during their lifetime or at death to take care of the people or causes that were important to them. This was the kind of touchy-feely conversation I imagine is more comfortable for female advisors than male advisors.

In these conversations, I have had male clients break down in tears as they talked about disappointments in life or failed expectations or any number of missed opportunities. They felt comfortable opening up because I provided a safe space for them to openly share their deepest emotions. I have not heard many stories about men doing this in front of other men; it just isn't done. I'm not sure that matters in the overall scheme of things, but it is quite a privilege to have a grown, successful man feel comfortable enough to be that vulnerable in your presence. It creates a bond that is not easily broken.

THE PSYCHOLOGY OF WORKING WITH MEN

I don't know how it is for other female advisors, but generally speaking, I found male clients easier to work with than female clients. I'm not sure why this was, but I don't think it's that much different than in other areas of life. It seems to me that men, typically, are just not as complicated as women. I always joke that most men are happy as long as they have a big screen TV and a remote control. My husband would add a cold beer to that equation, but that's about it! But that's not to say they don't have their own needs and expectations for the financial planning process.

While women tend to want financial security, men tend to be bigger risk-takers. They want to talk about the home runs; the big hit; the next big deal; or the double-, triple-, or ten-bagger. Just like they like to drive fast cars, men want their investments to be fast and furious. Why is that? In my opinion, the DNA of men and women is vastly different. (I use that term casually, not scientifically.)

From the dawn of civilization, men (in most hunter-gatherer societies, at least) have been assigned the role of hunter. Their job was to bring home the bacon. Her role was to fry it up in the pan. In many parts of the world today, this is still how things work. Regardless of how much has changed over the centuries, I still believe these differences are hardwired in men and women, to some degree. A man expects to go to work and be the provider. He has done it all his life and knows if the chips were down, he could do it again. That's why he isn't predisposed to worrying about running out of money. His internal DNA says if he runs out of money, he'll go make some more.

This is just not so for women. As I mentioned earlier, it has been well documented that women fear running out of money more than just about anything else. Hence, there's an art to working with couples. You have to address both of their deep-seated needs. If you only appeal to the woman and her need for safe, safe, safe, then you will bore the man to death. If you start talking about the next start-up opportunity or the new hot deal, then you may get interest from the man, but you will often lose the woman.

To overcome the inherent clash of needs, you have to acknowledge the differences in their inherent natures. You need to point blank tell the woman your plan is going to take care of her. She needs to know that all her security needs will be met. At the same time, you need to assure the man you will also meet his need to have some Vegas money or to drive in the fast lane. The sooner in the conversation you can bring these points to the forefront, the better; otherwise, you're going to lose one or the other of them.

As I said before, men do have fears. However, you will generally not get that from him in a meeting with his wife. Normally, the only time you'll get a sense of what the man fears is when he's by himself and you put him in a safe environment. What I have found from the many, many conversations I have had with male clients over the years is that even the most successful men fear disappointing the people around them, the people who depend on them. A lot of times, men feel that they've been put on a pedestal, and they're supposed to have made all the right decisions, all the right moves, and to be the caretakers of their families.

The last few financial crises have been very hard on men. They did their best to do well by their families, only to lose a lot of money in real estate and/or the stock market. So many men base their entire identity on their position as the leader of their family or the status of their job. When they lose a lot of money or feel they have made terrible mistakes (or worse yet, get fired), they fear the potential loss of status more than anything in the world. Overall, men don't require a lot to make them happy, but losing the respect of their families or status among their peers is a huge issue for most men. They will go to great lengths to protect themselves from that type of loss.

If you're a male advisor working with men, it's easy. You have such a clear advantage because men do business on the golf course and in other social settings. I've seen my male colleagues leave the office on Wednesday afternoons—the afternoon doctors traditionally take off—to pick up a golf game with a bunch of doctors. In general, I think you men are much better at networking with each other and setting up introductions. Men have no problem calling another man and asking for an introduction. I belonged to a couple of professional women's groups in Dallas, and we have often discussed this clear difference in the way men and women network. We decided there was significant value in having the "good old boy" network.

ADVICE FOR WOMEN ADVISORS

As a female advisor who was practically a pioneer in the financial service industry, I know only too well the advantages and disadvantages of being a woman in this business. In the course of my career, I generally refused to give in to any stereotypes about my place as a woman in the industry. I have never allowed myself to see or acknowledge a glass ceiling; in my mind, the only ceiling that existed was in my own head. Because I was an entrepreneur who never received a W-2 paycheck from an employer, my ability to make the same as any of my male counterparts was certainly within my own control. The fee schedules were the same; the payouts were the same, etc., so I never felt I couldn't compete on equal footing with men or make myself an even stronger competitor if I chose. That being said, there were some prospecting methods I felt were not well suited to me.

Let's take golf, for instance, which we know works so well for men. I admit I thought about taking up golf to meet potential clients but ultimately ruled it out. As a woman, I did not think it would be wise to show up at the golf course on an afternoon in the hopes of picking up a golf game as a fourth with a group of men. Why? First, having a woman join the game would likely change the nature of the men's experience on the course. Rather than being able to spit and cuss on the course (along with other things my husband said are probably not appropriate to mention in this book), most men would naturally clean up their act to accommodate a woman playing with them. They might not like that; after all, it's their afternoon to play and be "themselves." Second, if I did go golfing with three other men, I had to imagine their wives wouldn't be too excited to meet with me after that. I can just envision the conversation at home: "Honey, I met this amazing woman golfing today. She was out there by herself and happened to join the three of us men for a round of golf. Oh, by the way, she is a financial advisor, and I really think we should meet with her." I can only imagine the wife's response.

At one point, I did consider taking golf lessons and playing in the weekly women's nine-hole golf outing. Then I realized if I were going to do this, it would have to be solely for the love of the game, not because I wanted to use it as a prospecting tool to meet female clients. Why? Because there is an unspoken rule that would have likely worked against me. Care to guess what it is?

Let me give you a hint: What is the one question that's never asked of a woman by either a man or another woman?

Stumped? Most people are. I have noticed, however, that no one ever asks a woman, "What do you do?" It's completely taboo. That's because no one wants to put a woman in the position of possibly having to answer, "I don't do anything." Or "I'm a homemaker."

I have a funny sideline story to prove my point here. My husband and I have gone to five of his high school class reunions—the tenth, fifteenth, twentieth, thirtieth, and fortieth. When we left the last reunion, I told my husband I couldn't believe that, in all the reunions we attended, not one person I spoke to at any of the functions had ever asked me what I did for a living. They all knew my husband was an airline pilot, but not one of them knew about my work. They didn't ask! I'm a woman—I swear asking the question is still taboo!

In short, if you are a female financial advisor golfing with men or women, the topic of what you do for a living would likely never come up in conversation. You could force the topic in both situations, but I doubt it would be comfortable in either setting, and it just might be off-putting. That's why I suggest you only take up golf if you truly love the sport, and not because you think it would help you market yourself.

If you are a female advisor who works with or prospects to men, here's another "sand trap" that requires careful thought and a careful approach. If the man is a part of a couple and you want to do business with the couple, go out of your way to make sure the woman in the picture never feels threatened by you. I remember when I was a younger advisor in my early thirties. I wanted to cut my hair short and spikey and wear interesting, fashionable clothes, including short skirts, to the office. A mentor of mine said, "You know, Erin, it's your prerogative to wear what you want outside the office. However, inside the office there's too much at risk if you become a threat to anyone, especially to a man's wife or an office coworker."

I realized he was right. That was great advice. From that day forward, I went out of my way to dress very professionally, and one might add, a little on the "frumpy" side. As a result, I have never been a threat to a prospective female client. I could also count on the fact that my male prospects were looking at my eyes and listening to what I had to say, rather than distracted by cleavage or a short skirt. You certainly don't want the wife walking out thinking, "So, she wants my money and my husband!" That would not be conducive to your business relationship with any couple, so do not do—or wear—anything that could lead the woman to think this way.

OTHER PSYCHOLOGICAL FACTORS TO KEEP IN MIND

When dealing with prospects or clients, the maxim, KISS (Keep It Simple, Stupid) always makes sense. I spoke at length, earlier, about why it is so important to make sure you are using language that can be easily understood, no matter how little knowledge your prospects or clients have of financial planning. You never want to be condescending, but you also don't want to talk above anyone's head. That's not the way to impress people. In fact, you lose their attention and the opportunity to get the best outcome for your client.

Also be careful to not baffle clients or prospects with industry jargon. If you don't know the answer to a question, don't make it up. It's much better to say, "That's a great question and frankly, it's been a long time since anybody's asked me that. I'll refresh my memory (or find out the answer) and get back to you." Clients appreciate the fact that you don't know everything. Anybody who tries to come off as if they know everything is usually exposed quite quickly.

Again, there are times when it is to your advantage to play "dumb." As I said in chapter 6, I actually try to underwhelm clients with my own knowledge because I want them to lean on the members of my team, not me. Very often, I would end the first meeting with a prospect by saying, "Now you know everything I know! From this point forward, we'll bring in experts in all the areas that are relevant to your situation." I made it clear that the smartest thing I have ever done was to hire people smarter than me.

Clients are better served when they are not coming to you for everything. More to the point, that is the only way to build a business that can work without you. In the end, your responsibility as the founder and owner of the company is to make sure everything that is promised is done and done by people who have expertise in that particular area.

THE KEY TO IT ALL—TELL YOUR STORY

Clients will only do business with you and take your advice if they trust you and believe you always have their best interests in mind. As investment guru Nick Murray has often said, "Clients don't care what you know until they know that you care." I can't tell you how strongly I agree with those words. You really do have to care about the outcome for your clients. If you can't demonstrate that you care about their outcome, they aren't going to listen to anything you have to say.

One way to establish trust is to tell your own story. I tried to tell my story as early in the relationship as I could, for good reason. I realized in the course of our process, I was going to ask them a lot of very personal questions. I had to, in order to do a good job. If I was to protect them and find out what they cared about, I had to know nitty-gritty details about them, which many times includes the hidden dirty laundry known as family problems. Everyone has things they'd prefer to keep hidden; it's just a matter of how long it takes to uncover them.

The risk of not uncovering these hidden issues early in the relationship is that they will often come back and derail even the most meticulous plans you could have created to help your clients reach their financial goals. For instance, it would have been nice to know their son was in drug rehab; you could have set aside funds to handle future stays in rehab or other complications. It would have been nice to know that your client's mom was likely going to have to move in with them, which would require their current house to be retrofitted to accommodate her wheelchair. All those dirty laundry items have potential negative consequences for your clients' lifestyles.

I always told clients, "I don't like surprises. I want to make sure we have considered every single thing that could come along and derail your plans." That is easier to articulate, once you have opened up and told your own personal story and perhaps revealed a couple of crazy aspects about your life.

In the beginning, that wasn't so easy for me to do. If you read my personal story in chapter 1, you know that my early years were full of tragedy and misfortune. Once I got through that period, I did my best to forget all that had happened. As such, I never told my story to anyone—not my friends, or associates, and certainly not to prospective clients. I was ashamed of my personal background and didn't want people to know where I came from or how I got to this point. What a big mistake!

What caused me to tell my story was an actual prospect couple who came in and started describing what had recently happened in their family. Their son had been involved in a car accident with a motorcyclist in which someone was killed. I could see the toll this was taking on them. They felt guilt and fear. They were worried about losing their assets in a potential lawsuit, since the son had been driving their car. As I heard their story, I began to shake. It opened up an old wound and took me back in time, causing me to relive all those emotions. It felt like someone had just ripped a Band-Aid off an open sore. But I knew what I had to do. I had to tell them the same thing had happened to me. I had to share with them that while their son felt like he would never laugh again, he would. Time would heal those wounds.

I found myself going through the drama and the details of my story, but more importantly, I noticed an immediate change in their demeanor. I wasn't just some uninterested third-party consultant. I was sharing in their humanity. I was relating to them on a very deep and personal level. What I realized that day was that prospects and clients want to work with REAL people, not glitzy salespeople. They want to relate to an authentic, caring individual. Their money is *personal* to them, just as their hopes, dreams, and fears are. The sooner you can relate to them on a real and personal basis, the sooner they let down their guard. It is then that trust begins to take hold.

Here's another example: At one point, I was asked to meet with another financial advisor whom I did not know. I wasn't sure why we were meeting, but a client wanted me to meet her, so I agreed. When we walked into the restaurant, I could immediately sense that this woman was very intimidated by me. Her body language said it all; her hands were folded firmly across her chest, and she wouldn't look me in the eye. In our awkward first minutes, I found out she was divorced, and was a financial advisor who presumably specialized in working with other divorced women. That being said, it was like pulling teeth to get that information out of her.

When I tried to ask her some basic questions about her area of expertise, she gave me one-word answers. I still hadn't figured out why I was there, but I began to suspect that her friend may have thought I could be a good referral source for her or perhaps a mentor of sorts. Since she was so closed off to me, I figured that she was probably very closed off to her prospects and clients as well. I decided to try a little experiment and said, "Okay Kate, tell me about you, like how long were you married?" I was thinking since her expertise was supposedly in divorce matters, she must have been married—perhaps a good place to start. She responded by saying, "I don't think that's relevant or important."

Her answers to all my simple questions were borderline combative. It was clear I wasn't making any headway with her. Asking her questions wasn't going to help me develop this relationship; that was certain! I finally said, "Okay, maybe it would help you if I told you a little about me and my background." As I began telling my personal story, I could see her demeanor and body language change immediately. All her defenses came down and her arms opened up. A conversation began. Because I knew she was new to the business, I took the liberty of offering her some unsolicited advice. I said, "Kate, let me tell you what I just experienced in our meeting. When I arrived at this restaurant, you were clearly closed off to me, based on your obvious body language. You gave me one-word answers to everything I asked. Some of your responses were borderline combative. That was until I decided to take the first step in trying to form a relationship with you by opening up and telling you all the gory details of my life.

"Here's what I observed: Once I opened up to you, you felt comfortable. I let my guard down, so now you feel comfortable." She started nodding in agreement. I said, "Let me tell you something about growing a financial services business. You said you're trying to grow your practice and you want to work with divorced women. Don't you think they've experienced some of the same things you have, and don't you think the very first thing you're going to need to do is tell your story so they know you can relate to them? I can tell you right now, if you behave in the manner you just behaved with me, your career is never going to work. Your prospects will likely be just as closed down as you were with me. How are you going to help them if you can't get them to talk? You are going to have to be the first to take off all your proverbial clothes and expose yourself to your clients. I call this 'getting naked first.'"

Kate had an overwhelming reaction to my comments; she started crying. The idea of opening up and exposing herself to me, or to her future prospects, had never occurred to her. She said the idea was actually frightening. The story of her divorce was so painful to her, yet she quickly saw that allowing herself to be vulnerable would give her the greatest opportunity to actually relate to and eventually help her prospects. Since then, she has told me dozens of times how helpful that little piece of advice was for her. She admitted that she couldn't understand why female prospects were not opening up to her. She hadn't connected the dots. That was a huge breakthrough for my friend Kate.

EVERYONE HAS FEARS

Here is another example of the power of a personal story. At one point, I was given the opportunity to speak in Austin to a group of people whose minimum net worth was $50 million. They were members of a local group who met on a regular basis to hear new ideas. This day, I happened to be their speaker. From the moment I walked in, I sensed a really negative vibe. The body language of the attendees was so obviously closed off, I had to ask myself why they were even there. It was clear most of these people had been to dozens or hundreds of free lunches and dinners. Their body language told me they assumed they had heard every idea on the planet and they felt my speech was going to be another worthless presentation, as so many of the previous presentations had been. It was almost as if they were being polite just by attending. Mind you, I don't get opportunities to speak to one hundred people, all worth more than $50 million, all that often, so I was pretty intimidated. Fortunately, I had my silver bullet with me. I had my story.

After a brief but awkward start, I began telling my story. I talked about the fatal car accident I was in at age sixteen and my fear of being sued or worse, ending up in jail. I talked about my mother's fear of losing our only asset, our family home. I knew each of these people in the audience had a large net worth, they probably had children or grandchildren who drove cars or boats in their names, and they probably hadn't done adequate asset protection planning.

Fortunately, asset protection strategies were my topic for this speech. What is always interesting in our business is that regardless of the net worth of the person sitting in front of you, on the other end of that $50 million balance sheet is a real person. Once again, I watched the atmosphere in the room shift. Soon, audience members were engaged in my topic. It was as if they suddenly realized that essentially, we were all the same. Maybe they'd gotten lucky and their business had been successful, but they all had the same general fears. After the presentation, I had so many great conversations and wonderful feedback. I found out some of the people in that audience feared they might accidentally invest their money with the next Bernie Madoff. Some worried that leaving all their money to their children would ruin them. Some were worried to the point they had bodyguards to protect their children from being kidnapped.

Interestingly enough, they all had worries and fears in common; it was the type of things they worried about that were different. The bottom line: Everyone has fears. The degree to which you can connect with other people's humanity, including their unspoken fears, is the degree to which you have the basis for having truly authentic conversations and, ultimately, relationships. This is how to use psychology to create the optimal outcome for the client.

You need to be ready to tell a lot of stories. They need to be real stories; but keep in mind, *they don't have to be your own story*. Not everyone has a rags-to-riches story like mine. It doesn't matter. The stories just need to be relevant and to the point, not random or self-serving. The clients must be able to relate to those stories. Otherwise, it can be disastrous; so, don't pull stories out of your back pocket that are totally irrelevant to the discussion just for the sake of telling a story. My best advice is to pay attention along your journey so that you're picking up relevant stories that you can share with the next person down the line.

PERSONAL DISCIPLINE REQUIRED

It should probably go without saying that a tremendous amount of personal discipline and dogged determination are required to achieve a high level of success in our business. I'm sure that could be said about any industry. As I said earlier in this book, I realize not everyone wants to be at the top of the heap. For those who do want to make it to high levels in our business, the concept of personal discipline cannot be ignored. In fact, I believe it must be mastered. I had to create routines and rituals for me to stay focused because things like follow-through are not in my DNA and therefore not my strong suit. That being said, I was fortunate to have an internal combustion engine that thrived on achievement for achievement's sake, so it didn't take much to motivate me.

One thing I learned early was that I had to be very judicious with my time. When I started, I had a five-year-old at home and a husband who was commuting in and out of Panama City, Florida, from Dallas. Essentially, I was a single mom for the first couple of years in the business. I will go into the disciplines I established later on. But suffice it to say I was up early in the morning, took my son to his private school, and then began my day of prospecting. I knew every minute counted, so I tried to arrange meetings like my Out-to-Lunch Bunch for breakfast, lunch, cocktails, and/or dinners.

In the early years, cocktails and dinners were virtually out because I had to pick my son up from day care, but all other times in the day I had to be very focused. I was very serious about building my business. The one thing I did religiously was to leave my office by 4:30 p.m. each afternoon so I could pick my son up at the after-school day care center. More than anything in the world, I did NOT want my son to be the last child picked up. I can honestly say he never was.

Once I got home, I was "Mom" until 8:00 p.m. when he went to bed. From 8:00 p.m. on, I went back to work (from home), doing paperwork and following up on things from that day or the previous days. I would fall into bed around midnight and get up and do the same thing over again day after day, week after week. It took that kind of commitment to make it. I still think it takes that kind of commitment. I still work very hard and put in long hours, just in a different capacity. Today, I am just as committed to training advisors so they can build the businesses of their dreams.

SUNDAY NIGHT DISCIPLINE

If there was one discipline that I think made ALL the difference in the world, it was my Sunday night routine. To give you some background on how this ritual came to be, it is helpful to note that from the time my son was in junior high until he left for college, I cooked the same meal every Sunday night. He and his good friend, Whitney, convinced me to cook roast beef, mashed potatoes, gravy, and corn for anywhere between twelve and twenty-five people EVERY Sunday night.

The people who came were neighbors and friends. They knew to let me know by Saturday night if they would join us so I could take out one, two, or more roasts from the freezer. On Sunday morning before church, I would peel the potatoes and have them in a pot on the stove. After church, I took about a one-hour nap. The rule was—everyone came at 6:00 p.m. and left by 8:00 p.m. *with the dishes done.* Otherwise, I couldn't have pulled it off week after week. They also knew that five minutes after they left, our son went upstairs for the evening, and I went back to work.

I didn't leave my home, but I got out my briefcase and started planning for my next week. I would go through all my e-mails from the week before to be sure all of them had been answered. I would consolidate notes from my yellow legal pads and make sure I had downloaded all my meetings. I would gather up my receipts for lunches or dinners from the previous week and get them ready, with their appropriate IRS explanation, to give to my bookkeeper (who was my husband for a lot of years). I then got out a brand-new legal pad and started planning my week. I always had my top twenty prospects listed and my top twenty centers of influence to contact. The first page of my legal pad listed what I was going to do the following week; the pages after that were my questions or assignments for the team. My goal was to be completely finished and organized for the week by 11:00 p.m. I would then go outside and have a glass of wine and read something non-business related, like a cooking magazine, to take my mind off the work that lay ahead.

On Monday mornings, the alarm rang at 5:30 a.m. I have never worked out on Monday mornings; although, I have frequently attended evening yoga or other exercise classes. I left my home at 6:30 a.m. because I wanted to be the first one at the office and ready to rock and roll for the week.

For years, I first went to a Marriott Hotel next to my office, where I reviewed my notes and got ready for the week.

At precisely 8:00 a.m., our team would meet for an hour or more to go through the items listed on my pages and pages of notes. By the end of that meeting, the team knew what they were supposed to work on and what outcomes I expected to see. For me, the sense of confidence I gained by being one hundred percent organized every Monday morning was worth every minute

I spent on Sunday night. I couldn't have achieved what I have without that routine.

Years later, after my son left for college, I did not do the Sunday night dinners anymore. Instead, I began my workweek around 6:00 p.m. so I could finish closer to 10:00 p.m. Also, we transformed the Monday morning meetings substantially; eventually, all team members were responsible for being prepared for the week. I no longer came in and told them what they should do. In fact, we started the meeting thirty minutes later (at 8:30 a.m.), and a different team member led the meeting each Monday.

By 8:15 a.m., each team member was responsible for going into our hard drive to fill out what we called our "At a Glance." Each team member wrote what they did the previous week, and they wrote what they would be working on in the coming week. The business evolved enough that I didn't have to tell them what to do. We had professionals who knew the Steps of our Process and knew what they needed to get done. Nevertheless, it gave me confidence to see this sheet in writing by 8:30 a.m. every Monday morning. I knew every member of the team knew what they were supposed to do that week, and it gave me a chance to ask questions or redirect their time if I knew of a more pressing issue.

YOUR ULTIMATE OUTCOME IS UP TO YOU!

Within the first year, I learned many lessons, most of which were painful. One of the hardest things for me to wrap my arms around was that I was pretty much on my own to sink or swim. Thank God for my friend Hal, because he was not only my mentor but also my only real friend in the office. The other brokers initially liked me when I was new and non-threatening. They were as convinced as my manager that I was going to fail. After all, I was twenty-nine, female, blonde, and new in town. I swear the office staff took bets on my demise and went out of their way to help me reach that conclusion. I was never quite sure why people were so hell-bent on seeing me fail. It took many years before I figured it out.

The truth is that most people are satisfied with mediocrity and anyone who rises above mediocrity is seen as a threat. Most people are not willing to do what it takes to achieve tremendous, outrageous success. It is hard, and it takes too much effort. Most people choose the path of least resistance and bristle at anyone who chooses to go down the road less traveled. For whatever reason, I have always chosen the road less traveled. What I have found is that all the "goodies" are at the end of that path. However, choosing to do what others will not do can be rather lonely. There are not always a lot of cheerleaders along the way.

During the years I have counseled other producers, I have often made these two observations:

1. It is lonely at the top.
2. If it were easy, everyone would do it.

I don't know where you are in your career path. You may be satisfied with where you are and if so, congratulations! Keep doing whatever you are doing. On the other hand, you may wonder what it might be like to reach a higher level of productivity and financial success. You might be curious to find out what "goodies" are waiting at the other end of the rainbow. I'm not sure what drives you. For me, it was two things:

1. Being able to help our clients create or maintain their preferred lifestyles and, equally as important, helping them protect their legacy for their loved ones. Knowing how hard our clients have worked for their money and how much they love their families inspired me to do the very best I could and be the very best person I could become.

2. Having a lot of money to be able to help my family and contribute to the charitable causes I am passionate about. Being able to influence the outcomes and the lives of others who have not had the advantages I have been afforded was a huge motivator.

For more information and additional resources, go to www. erinbotsford.com.

QUESTIONS TO PONDER:

- **Do you really understand the mindset of the client sitting in front of you?**

At the end of the day, your job is to get the client to say "yes" to your recommendations. Presumably, your recommendations are the precise prescription to get the clients to the place they told you they wanted to go. To get there, they need to take action. It is your job to help move them along that path. Consider making the journey a collaboration between the clients and you.

- **Are you telling your story, or other people's stories, so that your clients can relate to you?**

To connect with other people's humanity, you may need to show your vulnerable side first. Telling your story (if it's relevant and not self-serving) is one way to do that.

- **What are your weekly rituals that will keep you disciplined?**

You cannot grow a large practice or reach higher goals unless you are personally disciplined. I will restate: My Sunday night ritual was probably the single greatest step in making sure I hit the ground running on Monday morning. Setting up your personal rituals and disciplines cannot be overstated.

CHAPTER 9

TIME TO GIVE BACK

GIVING BACK TO THE INDUSTRY

People often ask me if I regret selling my firm in 2017 and every time I say, "Absolutely not." Why? Because now I am free to share all of the wisdom I learned along the way and I have become a "force multiplier," which is the greatest reward of all. As in all things in my business and in my life, the next steps in my career were not planned per se but instead came as a natural next step.

As you can imagine, once I made it to *Barron's* Top 100 list a few times, I naturally got asked to give industry speeches. Because of the limits on my time, I would always say yes to one or two a year.

In early 2016, I was asked to give six speeches in a short period of time and at first, I turned them down. They were paying a good bit of money for each one-hour speech, but I thought: "It's never a one-hour speech. It's a day to travel there, a day to do the speech, and then a day to travel home." While the speaking fee was large in relative terms, I told my husband: "I could get on the phone and call a client and make that amount of money. I don't have to get on a plane to do so."

Shortly after I made that statement, one night I woke up and thought: "What if, every time I got on a plane to give a speech, we would give half of the speaking fee to the orphanage we were supporting?" I talked to my husband about the idea, and he agreed it could be a game changer in our ability to give to the causes we cared about. Because of that one idea, my entire attitude changed. I now had dual purposes to get on a plane: the ability to give back to the industry that allowed me to become successful AND the means to feed more and more kids. It made all the difference in the world.

The night before my first speech, I woke up and had an idea. I created a new slide deck that read: "Come spend the day with me and my team." I had eighteen advisors sign up the next day, each agreeing to pay $3,000 for the day experience. Half of that would go to the orphanage we supported as well.

Truth be told, I didn't have a program of any kind created for them. I remember going back to my office in a panic and saying: "We have eighteen advisors coming next month; we need to come up with a plan!" I did come up with a program and for a couple of years we had between fifteen and twenty advisors come through our office each quarter. I had each member of my team give them a briefing on what they did for our firm, and I gave them as much as I could in one day. I knew they left my firm overwhelmed by all they had learned, so I also gave them two hours of time with any member of my team. The caveat was: They had to submit their questions in advance.

After a while, it was apparent *they all had the same questions.* A question kept lingering in my head: "Is there a way to create something for advisors where I could teach them absolutely everything I had learned in my three decades in business? After all, it seemed like it would have been such a waste to just walk away from the business and keep everything I learned along the way in my head." I kept wondering: "Does everyone have to make ALL the mistakes I made? Could I make the journey a little easier on advisors so they don't have to make all the same mistakes?"

Ultimately, I wanted to give back to the industry that allowed me, a poor, broken girl, to achieve a ridiculous amount of success in this business.

So, I created what is now known as the Elite Advisor Success System™. It is a complete online course where advisors can truly learn everything they need to know to create the business of their dreams. They don't have to travel to learn what I know; they have access to the learning 24/7. Literally, while they walk their dog, drive to their next appointment, or walk on the treadmill, they can learn what to do, and equally important, what not to do!

Today, my "WHY"—what drives me—is *their success*. In fact, every time I interact with my advisors, I tell them their success is the oxygen that feeds my soul! And I'm serious about that. I live for their success stories and the good news is, I get e-mails or texts with success stories almost every single day!

One recent story was from a guy who started in my Elite Advisor Success System™ just a year and a half ago. He had never charged a financial planning fee. His first fee was $1,250 and his wife chastised him for charging it, saying she was fearful he'd blow up his business. A few short months later, I received a text from him that he quoted and received a financial planning fee of

$125,000! (I bet his wife is not complaining today!) Those are the stories that feed my soul.

You can find out more about this course, that has changed the lives of MANY advisors, by going to www.erinbotsford.com.

QUESTIONS TO PONDER:

- **What about you? What drives you?**

- **What's your WHY?**

- **What do you want for your business and your life?**

I raised these questions in chapter 1, and I am returning to it here because it's *that important.* You must figure out what you're going to do with the money you earn and what impact you want to have; that's what keeps you focused. Without that, you'll peter out in a hurry. The winds of discouragement will blow you over unless you are *passionately committed to something bigger than yourself.*

If you have a big enough WHY to sustain you, then it's easier to keep your momentum. So, figure out what will drive you when the going gets tough. If you are very clear about that, then the rest is easy.

PLANNING AND EXECUTING YOUR EXIT

BEGIN WITH THE END IN MIND (STEPHEN COVEY)

As I've mentioned earlier, I sold my firm in October 2017 in an all-cash transaction. I had three offers on the table and was able to choose the one I wanted. People have asked me what led up to my sale, what went right, what went wrong, what would I do differently, and essentially how I prepared my business for the best outcome.

After thirty-one years in the business, I was ready to sell. Having built a multi-million-dollar firm, having reached the *Barron's* Top 100 list more times than I could count, I had achieved well more than I could have ever imagined, especially considering where I started. I kept thinking: "I've been working since I've been eleven years old; is there something else I could do and get as much satisfaction?"

As I said earlier, it turns out my advisor training business has been thousand times more satisfying because, to me, it feels like a force multiplier. I don't just get to help the clients of my firm; I get to help train thousands of advisors and impact how they do business with all their clients. It's been such a win for me and, hopefully, for the advisors who have gone through my training program.

That said, to me, from the first day you are in business, I think you should be asking yourself: "What do you want to have happen on the last day you're in this business?" In other words, what do you want your end game to look like? Do you want to get a big check like I did and be able to walk away? Do you want to leave your business to a son or daughter? Do you want to hand it over to your team as your succession plan? What exactly does that day look like?

Thinking through that question is probably the MOST important question an advisor should ponder, and the sooner you start thinking about the outcome you want, the better. Truth be told, your outcome on that last day will largely be affected by what your business looks like on that last day. As I've said earlier and will say again and again, if your business is dependent upon you meeting with all or most of your existing clients, it will have very little value in the marketplace. Why? Because the risk of clients walking away after a transaction will be priced into the value you receive.

Case in point: In case you missed it in chapter 2, the day I sold my firm to another advisory practice, the buyer of my firm purchased another woman's firm. I am told she had about the same amount of assets under management (AUM) as me and the same number of clients. Unfortunately for her, she had two things going against her: First, all her clients were used to (and expected) to meet with her, and second, she had a massive stroke and HAD to sell. Hence, because of the dependency of the clients on meeting with her, that risk was priced into the purchase price she received. I am told by reliable sources she received approximately twenty-five cents/dollar compared to me.

Given the choice, I'll assume that's not an outcome you'd be happy with.

The sad thing about that outcome is that it was totally avoidable. Perhaps the stroke was not avoidable; none of us is guaranteed tomorrow. But setting your business up so it doesn't depend totally on you for meeting with every single client for every meeting IS the key to preventing this type of negative financial outcome.

That said, getting a full-price offer doesn't happen by accident. In my case, it was a very planned outcome. I wanted to protect the value of my firm for me, for my husband, and for my son. Early on, I protected the value of my work with life insurance; eventually, I protected the value by getting the business to the point where it ran without my day-to-day involvement.

THE BEGINNING OF THE END

I started thinking about my exit the day I left Paul's office in 2000. As I said earlier, Paul gave me a few assignments and I tackled them with vigor. The first was to read the book *The E-Myth Revisited,* by Michael Gerber. I picked it up at the Washington, DC airport and read it on the plane ride home. I still have that original marked-up, highlighted, underlined copy.

Reading that book turned on a couple of light bulbs in my head. First, I realized most successful businesses *hire* people to do the actual work of the business. The owner of McDonald's hires high school kids to do the work of that business (flipping and serving burgers). The CEO of UPS hires drivers to do the work of that business. In most small businesses, the owner hires other people to do the work of the business. Plumbing supply company owners hire plumbers to go to peoples' houses and fix their plumbing. Electricians do the same thing.

Even in other professional services businesses, the partners or owners hire others to do the work. Attorneys have paralegals and CPAs hire junior accountants. The bottom line is that in an established business, the owner typically doesn't do all of the actual work of the business.

It was a hard realization that I didn't really have a business. I just had a job with a very friendly boss . . . ME. I was doing everything in the business. I was the salesperson, the technician, and the manager. The good news is, at the time, I only had one person to manage and that was me!

Michael Gerber's advice was to start thinking of my business as part of a franchise and imagine I was opening the first office. In my financial services franchise, I had to hire people to do the technical work of the business, I had to create systems and processes for those people so they would know what I wanted them to do in the business, etc.

In chapter 7, I went through how I finally created my systems and process manual (when my assistant was out with her dying husband). From that point on, every employee who came on board had to update the systems and process manual so that pretty much anyone could come in and do the work of the business.

Depending upon the role for which they were hired, I needed them to be able to do things like place trades, create forms, create financial plans, send out birthday cards and/or gifts, schedule appointments, arrange for seminars or any number of other events, and greet and seat prospects and clients. Eventually, they needed to know how to meet alone with clients and conduct reviews.

SETTING THE GOAL

I know a big factor in my successful exit was being a dedicated and diligent goal setter. One of the goals I wrote down on my plane ride home from my day with Paul was that *someday* I wanted to have two offices with a total of seven conference rooms, filled with clients of my firm, and I wasn't in any of them.

That's exactly what happened. In hindsight, I wish I could have written down even bigger goals. I now know that your brain has to stay consistent with what you tell it, so I wish I had written that I wanted to have ten offices with forty conference rooms, filled with clients of my firm . . . because I now know I would have been forced by my brain to find a way to make that happen.

LEVERAGE IS THE KEY TO GETTING A HIGH MULTIPLE

If I've said this once, I've said it a thousand times. If your business depends on you to meet with every client for every review meeting, it will have very little value in the marketplace. Oh, sure, you'll get something for your business but it likely won't be much.

There's too much risk for a buyer to buy a practice where the clients are dependent upon the advisor. When the advisor is gone, then what?

To get a high multiple for your business, you will need to hire and build at least a small team. Think about this: You have to get to a point where someone else can replace you in the room and give advice to your clients. The more of those people you can hire and train, the bigger multiple you will get. That step alone reduces the risk to the buyer because clients are used to working with more than just you.

In my training program, I have an entire course designed to teach advisors who to hire, how to hire them, how to train them, and how to compensate them so they'll jump through fiery hoops for you and your business. I also train the exact steps you can use to completely transform your business into a self-managing company in three years. I suppose it can be done in less time but that's what I did it in and it's what the advisors I train have been able to do.

THE STEPS OF MY EXIT PROCESS

Truth be told, back in the day, there was little, if any, training on how to have a successful exit. Yes, there were companies out there like FP Transitions who would work with you when you were ready to sell, but I wanted a sneak preview LONG before I was ready to sell, to see what my business needed to look like to get the best price.

Since there wasn't a lot of training, I decided to "pretend" I was selling my business as early as 2002, which was fifteen years before

I actually sold. I met with a business broker and he lined up a few potential buyers. The process was fascinating, and I'd encourage anyone to do this. I was given checklists of things the potential buyers wanted to see.

They were normal things like my financial statements, organizational charts, roles and responsibilities of team members, and breakdown of assets under management by client (we removed the clients' names). One of them sent me a seventeen-page Word document with items they wanted to see.

My first reaction was: "I am NOWHERE NEAR ready to sell." My financials were messy. I'm embarrassed to admit I was writing checks for my nail appointments out of my business account! After all, it was just me and I owned it all but WOW . . . my eyes were opened.

In addition, the biggest question the buyers had was, how long would I stay on, and over what period of time would I be willing to basically float them a loan so they could buy my business? I didn't expect that! They all wanted to pay me out over time but have me actually continue to work in the business.

Why? Because the business was still WAY too dependent upon me. Going through that exercise was a wake-up call for me. While I turned down their paltry offer, I got to work on cleaning things up. I used their checklists to start assembling all the data a potential buyer would one day want.

Most importantly, I decided I needed to embrace the idea of leverage a lot more than I had been. I had a few people working for me at the time, but I had not empowered them. They were glorified "assistants," but they were not really responsible for meeting with clients, making recommendations, and essentially running all aspects of the business.

I spent the next ten years working on those items until my business ran one hundred percent without my day-to-day involvement. I started writing this book and, to prove to myself that my company could run without me, I took six months off in 2015. I went to India for a month, China for a month, Africa for a month, and then took the summer off. I went to the other ends of the earth so when I was awake the office was closed and vice-versa.

That year my firm had a record year! I had done it! I had a self-managing company that had two offices (Dallas and Atlanta), with seven conference rooms filled with clients of my firm, and eighteen employees to service those clients. I had worked myself out of a job, which was a pretty amazing feeling. I finally had a bona fide BUSINESS!

I still loved to "hunt" and that ended up becoming my only role in the firm. Someone else on my team ran every other element, from client meetings, HR, compliance, investment manager selection, and bookkeeping. Everything ran without me.

By the end of 2016, I had several firms reach out to me as potential buyers. I wasn't sure I wanted to sell but already I was enjoying my "Spend the Day" training sessions, pouring into advisors who were on the same journey I had been on. I loved watching their eyes light up as they learned what *could* be accomplished in this business.

In 2017, I decided to take the leap of faith and accept one of three offers. It was an all-cash offer and did not require any "look backs" (which many buyers require). A lot of times the buyer will want to "look back" twelve months after the sale to re-calculate the value, based on any assets lost due to clients leaving over the year. I did not have to agree to that because there was little, if any, risk of clients leaving. NO client on the books ever expected to meet with me. I sold the philosophy of my firm, not me. That policy alone paid big dividends in the end.

I was lucky. I picked the right buyer. He kept all my employees and as of the date of this writing, pretty much all of the clients are still on the books.

I don't know where you are in your journey. I hear advisors who say they never want to sell but I always wonder why they'd make that statement. After all, we teach and help other people make money by buying assets. Our businesses can be our single greatest asset; why would we not want to capitalize on that asset?

Then too, I realize some advisors make that statement because they know they have a firm that would likely not command much, in terms of price, because it's WAY too dependent on the advisor. Typically, the advisor knows that, but they are unwilling to do the work to make it attractive to a future buyer. I can't say I blame them, but I wish I could convince that advisor it's not hard when someone like me gives you the formula.

Also, not wanting to sell your business is fine as long as you can always work and you save a lot of money along the way in case you are not able to work, as was the case of the woman I mentioned earlier. As I said, she received twenty-five cents on the dollar compared to me, purely because her clients were all dependent on meeting with her and unfortunately, she'd had a massive stroke and had to sell.

I didn't want that outcome for me or my family. I also don't want that as an outcome for any advisor I work with. There's no excuse when there's a clear path to follow. Being a pioneer in this industry, I forged that path and now all you have to do is follow it.

For those who do want to sell one day, I applaud you. It's the greatest feeling in the world to receive a multi-million-dollar check that acknowledges the work you've put into building your business and the value you've created in the world.

Wherever you are on your business journey, I hope that by reading this book, you will be encouraged and inspired to take whatever the next step is for you. Trust me when I tell you ALL the goodies really are at the end of that proverbial rainbow.

I'd love to walk with you on your journey.

To find out more about our programs, go to www.erinbotsford.com.

QUESTIONS TO PONDER:

- **Have you planned your exit?**

  We all think we get to decide the date, time, price, and terms of our exit, but sometimes unexpected things happen that derail the best-laid plans. Have you done exhaustive planning for all contingencies that could happen in or to your business? We are planners, after all. We typically do great planning for our clients but can be woefully underprepared ourselves.

- **How much leverage do you have in your business?**

  If your business depends upon you meeting with every client, it will have very little value in the marketplace. What steps have you taken or will you take to ameliorate that risk?

ABOUT THE AUTHOR

Erin Botsford—advisor, author, and trainer, known as The Advisor Authority™

Having spent thirty-one years in the financial services business and achieving at the highest levels (*Barron's* Top 100 in all categories—Independent, Advisor, and Women Advisor), Erin sold her business in 2017 in a successful exit—a step most advisors want to achieve at the end of their careers.

Today, she is the creator of the **Elite Advisor Success System™**—a system that teaches advisors how to quickly grow their businesses exponentially and build firms that have all the elements needed for a future succession or exit. Her program delivers the five keys to business success in easy-to-understand modules; in less than six months, advisors can learn what might otherwise take them decades to figure out on their own.

Erin believes in the power of "modeling" and allows advisors to simply copy her success blueprint. Erin is also the author of two books, the first edition of *Seven Figure Firm: How to Build a Financial Services Business that Grows Itself* and *The Big Retirement Risk: Running Out of Money Before You Run Out of Time.*

With thirty-one years of field experience and an authentic personal story, she can relate to advisors at all levels. An international speaker, Erin shares her years of wisdom at industry conferences worldwide. To find out more, check out www.erinbotsford.com.

www.ingramcontent.com/pod-product-compliance
Lightning Source LLC
Chambersburg PA
CBHW030507210326
41597CB00013B/820